Deficit

Deficit

HOW FEMINIST ECONOMICS CAN CHANGE OUR WORLD

EMMA HOLTEN

Translation from the Danish
by Sherilyn Hellberg

WH Allen

UK | USA | Canada | Ireland | Australia
India | New Zealand | South Africa

WH Allen is part of the Penguin Random House group of companies
whose addresses can be found at global.penguinrandomhouse.com

Penguin Random House UK
One Embassy Gardens, 8 Viaduct Gardens, London SW11 7BW

penguin.co.uk
global.penguinrandomhouse.com

Originally published in Denmark as *Underskud* by Politikens Forlag in 2024
This edition published by WH Allen in 2025

1

Copyright © Emma Holten 2025
Translation © Sherilyn Hellberg
The moral right of the author has been asserted.

Poem extract on page 275 taken from *IT* by Inger Christensen, translated by Susanna Nied,
copyright ©1969 by Inger Christensen, Translation copyright © 2005, 2006 by Susanna Nied.
Reproduced with kind permission from Carcanet Press and by permission of
New Directions Publication Corp.

Penguin Random House values and supports copyright. Copyright fuels
creativity, encourages diverse voices, promotes freedom of expression and supports
a vibrant culture. Thank you for purchasing an authorised edition of this book and
for respecting intellectual property laws by not reproducing, scanning or distributing
any part of it by any means without permission. You are supporting authors and
enabling Penguin Random House to continue to publish books for everyone.
No part of this book may be used or reproduced in any manner for the purpose
of training artificial intelligence technologies or systems. In accordance with
Article 4(3) of the DSM Directive 2019/790, Penguin Random House expressly
reserves this work from the text and data mining exception.

Typeset by Jouve (UK), Milton Keynes

Printed and bound in Great Britain by Clays Ltd, Elcograf S.p.A.

The authorised representative in the EEA is Penguin Random House Ireland,
Morrison Chambers, 32 Nassau Street, Dublin D02 YH68.

A CIP catalogue record for this book is available from the British Library

Hardback ISBN 9780753561461
Trade Paperback 9780753561478

Penguin Random House is committed to a sustainable future for our business, our readers
and our planet. This book is made from Forest Stewardship Council® certified paper.

To Maria Cariola,
who is so good at laughing and thinking.

CONTENTS

Introduction   1

Chapter 1: A Mechanical Universe   25
Chapter 2: Who Gets to be Free?   49
Chapter 3: Through the Eye of a Needle   69
Chapter 4: What are We Worth?   91
Chapter 5: Worthless Maintenance   119
Chapter 6: Power Struggles   159
Chapter 7: Isolated Optimisation   195
Chapter 8: A Disservice to Public Services   221
Chapter 9: Beating Hearts in a Broken System   253

Conclusion   275

Acknowledgements   285
Notes   287
Illustration Credits   313
Index   314
About the Author   328

INTRODUCTION

In 2019, I was admitted to Bispebjerg Hospital in Copenhagen. I suffer from a chronic autoimmune condition called ulcerative colitis. My body attacks itself. The disease is unpredictable and strange, and no one knows exactly why I have it. Outbreaks can be triggered by stress, certain foods and also – unfortunately – by too much wine. When I found out I was ill, I realised that my mind and my body were one. If I'm sad, stressed, or exhausted, I get sick. No one knows what my immune system has in store for me, my community or those who love me.

In 2020, a year after I was hospitalised, the magazine *Mandag Morgen* published an article: 'Women continue to be net expense for the state'.[1] It was the sequel to a seven-year-old hit, 'Women are a deficit to society', which was published by the Danish Broadcasting Corporation in 2013.[2]

Mandag Morgen's article caught my eye. These headlines aren't so different from many others about economics. They appear objective and logical. Value is described as the result of a calculation, as a question with a simple answer. Who could disagree that women leech off the state coffers?

The numbers cited in the article were from the Danish Ministry of Finance. The ministry's method was quite simple: they calculated the value of women's contribution to the state by looking at their tax payments versus the costs of the services they receive during a lifetime and compared that to men's. Women got more than they gave, the article said: they took more parental leave, mothers frequently worked part time, and typically worked lower paying jobs in the public sector. They also 'drained' the public sector by tending to do expensive things like give birth. Denmark would be richer if women's lives looked more like men's, the experts concluded.

Due to their convincing form, these types of calculations have seeped into our culture and conversations. In 2024, it was reported that a candidate for Reform UK wrote on a message board two years earlier that he was sick of all this complaining from 'the sponging gender'. The reason he gave was simple economics: 'Men pay 80% of tax – women spend 80% of tax revenue. On aggregate as a group, you only take from society.' According to him, women were 'subsidised by men to merely breath [sic]'.[3]

The people who had cared for me at Bispebjerg Hospital were, by his logic and the ministry's, part of the problem. They worked in the public sector, many of them not making much money. The value of the work they had done was measured by the price of their labour; their work wasn't seen as creating value. This stunned me. They had saved my life. Every penny I earned from here on out was a direct consequence of their work.

Something was wrong. I felt we were looking at value in a distorted way. How did the economists in the Danish state reach a conclusion like this, and how had it become so widely accepted that it could go completely unchallenged, as if it were objective fact? This book seeks to answer that question. It's the history of how one very specific way of looking at value has trumped all others. You might feel that economics only impacts your life when you get paid or you visit your bank. But every single waking hour of your day is shaped by calculations coming from the state. Every profession, activity, product and relationship is part of what we call 'the economy', and is assigned a number, which represents its value. Understanding how this system works means pulling back the curtain on the decisions and ideas that have made our societies what they are today. The system can seem impossible to challenge. But I promise you, it is not.

THE LANGUAGE OF POWER

Economics is the mother tongue of politics. It is the language of power. No other way of thinking comes close to having the influence that economic concepts do. What we can *afford* has become the same as what is *possible*.

Like the headlines framing women as an economic burden, economic language can seem straightforward. We sometimes speak as if somewhere, a group of people with exceptionally strong Excel skills can answer a simple yes or no to the question of whether we can afford to staff hospitals better. It isn't so surprising that we think this. Thanks in part to the media, which loves nothing more than yes or no answers and official-looking graphs, we've been deluded into seeing economics as an exact science without any real internal debate. Many people would probably be surprised to learn that economists disagree about what money is, what banks do, what productivity means, and what inflation entails. In fact, in my work with economics, it has been difficult for me to find even a single thing that all economists agree on. Two of the world's most famous economists, Paul Krugman and Gregory Mankiw, disagree about the fundamental issue of whether or not rich people have earned their money in a legitimate way.[4] Every single day, there is disagreement about the past, present and future.

This debate is good, I think. This is how it should be in a social science dedicated to the study of people and our behaviour. And yet, we find ourselves part of a public discourse in which we are constantly presented with definitive economic answers, as if this disagreement didn't exist.

This is because there is one line of economic thinking that dominates all the others. It is most present in public institutions, in organisations such as the European Union and in the media. Its dominance is evident in the fact that it can state its conclusions without needing to account for the assumptions it has made about value, society and justice. We almost never see these assumptions laid out; they operate behind apparently neutral numbers. I have chosen to call this dominant form of economics 'established economics'.

Besides the ideas championed by established economics, there are tons of alternative ways of thinking at play in universities, in books and debates; many of these are included in this book. But to the great disappointment of all the exciting economists who have developed different visions and methods, their influence on the actual organisation of society is extremely limited. As the economist Diane Coyle writes in her book *Cogs and Monsters*, there is always a delay between academic work and what gets applied in practice.[5]

The economist Joan Robinson once said, 'The purpose of studying economics is not to acquire a set of ready-made answers to economic questions, but to learn how to avoid being deceived by economists.'[6] Every day, many of us are deceived by established economics. Even prime ministers, journalists and CEOs. Even economists.

FIGHTING TOOTH AND NUMBERS

The first reason that we have an established way of economic thinking (and thousands of unestablished ones) is because economic debate is a power struggle. The economist Paul Samuelson once said that he didn't care who wrote a nation's laws, as long as he got to write its economics textbooks.[7] Smart guy. The discipline that defines what has worth is the discipline that shapes the future. For that reason, many people throughout history have fought to have their particular economic analysis be considered 'true'.

The second reason is that politics creates a high demand for precise answers. Once we have a dominant narrative in place, it becomes difficult to challenge, creating a tough environment for the more sidelined forms of economics. There's nothing politicians love more than saying 'My plan will create 3,500 new jobs!' or 'My plan will save the state 8 million dollars!' There's something comforting about these claims, for both the citizen and the politician. The future can feel frightening, and numbers signal that *we've got it under control*. The correct decision is always just a calculator away. Established economics has been excellent at getting its answers to appear precise and scientific.

But this authority is a false one. No one knows what will happen in 2030. No one knows what will happen in six months.

The methods that economists have developed have given them unparalleled political power. There is no doubt that economics is the most powerful discipline in modern politics, regardless of which domain is under analysis.[8] Who wouldn't be tempted by the promise of a science that can speak with authority on such diverse things as elder care and shipping containers?

Economists' answers to the tasks and questions posed to them by politicians are presented as neutral assessments. All over the world there are offices devoted to state finances and well-funded economic councils, but we rarely hear about sociological or anthropological councils. The sociologists Marion Fourcade, Etienne Ollion and Yann Algan, who study the power of economic language, have called this 'the superiority of economists'. There's double entendre here: economists have more power relative to other social sciences. But this power has also given them substantial 'self-confidence' – a self-confidence that sometimes exceeds its limits.[9]

When the Danish government set up expert groups in 2021 and 2023 to look at climate taxes and employment reforms respectively, over half of the members of the group were economists, and there were no members with a background in natural or social science. Economists are also the only people who can become 'wise men' in the Danish Economic Council, which evaluates the consequences of Danish policy. According to the wise men themselves, their analyses are 'an independent contribution to the decision-making basis for economic policy.'[10] In 2013, the daily newspaper *Information* reviewed the Economic Council's growth forecasts and found that only one out of 35 turned out to be accurate.[11] When you read a newspaper headline about what something 'costs' the state, this number usually comes from these offices. The calculations and conclusions are rarely legitimately challenged – at least not publicly.

WHY FEMINIST ECONOMICS?

Since the 1960s, feminist economics has challenged the established notions of value, setting their sights especially on what is called reproduction: all the paid and unpaid activities it takes to keep people healthy, happy and alive. In this book, I have defined these activities broadly, including everything from the state school system to comforting a friend who's just been dumped. Reproduction is any act where at least two people in one way or another transform each other's minds or bodies. They leave the interaction somehow changed: more healthy, happy and alive. I use the words reproduction and care work (and occasionally maintenance) to describe these activities.

We often talk about care work as something that only sick people, old people, disabled people and children need. Feminist economics sees things differently: for us, caring for each other is a constant in all our lives. It is a prerequisite for us all being here, even in periods when we're healthy and apparently self-sufficient. No one can exist without, at some point, being taken care of and treated as valuable by other people. Caring is the work that makes all other work possible. This is a core belief of feminist economics, and as we'll see, it is a radical economic position.

It's not called feminist economics because only women benefit from understanding who has access to receiving care, who performs it, and how we value it. It's called feminist economics because women, for better or for worse, have always spent more time on these activities. Care affects us all, because it shapes our bodies, minds, homes, workplaces and the entire state.

If you are looking for a book with concrete tips on how to make your husband do the dishes more, this one isn't for you (unless, like me, you find tremendous self-help in the explanatory power of historical insights and political analyses. Then this book is perfect for you!). My gaze is fixed on the systems within which we all make decisions. It makes no difference to me whether you're a stay-at-home parent, an entrepreneur or happily childless. Regardless, you are a person who has both received and given care during your life. The circumstances under which we care for each other's bodies and minds aren't a given – it is an eternal struggle both to be able to care and to refuse to do so.

In this book, it might seem like only cisgender women, cisgender men and heterosexual nuclear families exist. This is due to how established economics has dealt with gender. With its devotion to neutrality and mathematics, economics has struggled to relate to the diversity of bodies and has had difficulty acknowledging the existence of discrimination and inequality. We don't all have the same starting point or the same bodies, but established economics has created and used a rigid concept of the 'normal' person. Therefore, established economics has also struggled to account for how the workforce is produced, where it comes from and what it requires to exist. But that doesn't mean that economics is irrelevant for those who do not identify with heteronormative understandings of gender and family. Quite the opposite! Producing labour power has always been a key economic question. Therefore, many of the cultural clampdowns on childless cis women, trans people, queer life, and alternative family forms have been supported by thinly veiled economic arguments that these people do not fulfil their reproductive obligations (a recent vice-presidential candidate in the United States called democrats with no children 'a bunch of childless cat ladies who are miserable at their own lives and the choices that they've made and so they want to make the rest of the country miserable, too')[12]. Therefore, what we consider to be a correct man, a woman, and a family is very much an economic issue. A nuclear family with a primary breadwinner and a secondary caregiver in paid work is an economic vessel as well as a source of love and care.

From an established economic perspective, the nuclear family is a highly cost-effective way to create new labour: it can hardly be cheaper to acquire new citizens than it is in this constellation. There are clear roles and as few hours and adults involved as possible. Regardless of your gender, sexuality or family form, you will find that anything that doesn't fit into the nuclear family constantly encounters institutional and cultural resistance in society as it stands today. You can switch things up a bit: maybe the straight man is the primary caregiver, maybe there are two same-sex parents. But the economy disciplines us. When care is deemed worthless, as few hours as possible should be spent on it.

Denmark is one of the world's most gender-equal countries, but the reality is that women here spend on average 54 minutes more than men working in the home every single day. Women work 3.5 hours in the home per day, men about 2.5.[13] And this doesn't include the *mental load*, which is the time spent planning, researching and organising the day-to-day running of the household. If you are not Danish, the numbers are probably more unequal where you live. Globally, 708 million women say that the reason they are not in paid work is because of care responsibilities. This is the case for only 40 million men.[14] Seventy-five per cent of the world's housework is performed by women.[15]

Graphs showing how earnings change after the birth of a first child. In every country across the globe, the penalty is larger for women. For most men, having children does not decrease your income; in some places, it might even increase it. Graphs adapted from a paper by Henrik Kleven et al: 'Child Penalties across Countries: Evidence and Explanations', AEA Papers and Proceedings, Vol. 109, 2019.

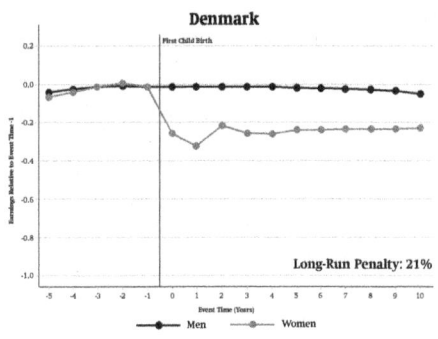

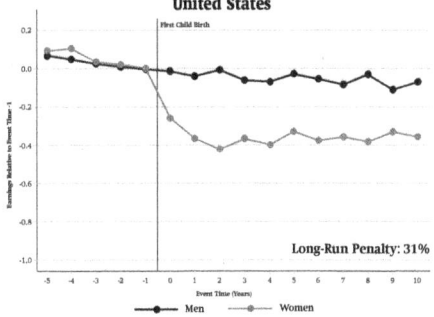

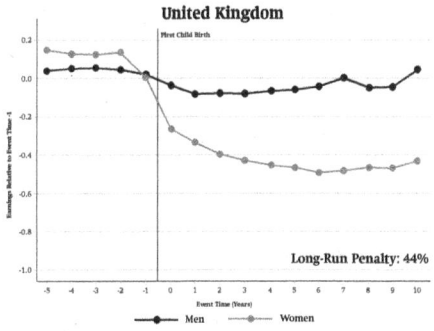

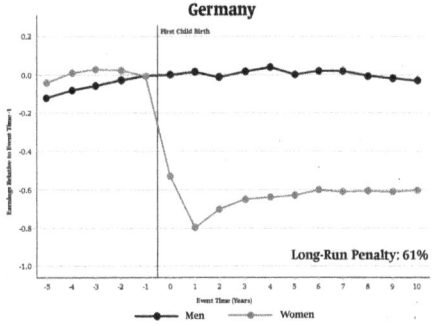

The extra hour that Danish women spend in the home each day adds up to nine weeks of full-time work more than men each year. Of course, much of this has to do with children. On average, the lifetime income of a Danish woman drops around 20 per cent after having her first child, which has serious consequences for their economic freedom and pensions.[16] In the European Union, the income that is 'lost' to women as a result of unpaid caretaking is around 242 billion euros each year.[17] Men's work hours, meanwhile, remain almost the same after having kids. There are two tragedies in this statistic. Performing unpaid care work is not just a burden but also a gift. And as it stands, both the burdens and the gifts are very unequally distributed.

If we turn to the paid sphere, women make up 80 per cent of all employees in the Danish social work and healthcare sector.[18] In the European Union, women make up 76 per cent of everyone who works with in the care sector.[19] Globally, the care sector consists of 249 million women and 132 million men.[20]

Women all over the world simply spend more time taking care of other people, both at home and at work, both when they are being paid, and when they are not. The mother tongue of politics struggles not only to understand the value of caring for one another, it struggles to understand the value of much of what makes life worth living.

THE PRICE OF EVERYTHING AND THE VALUE OF NOTHING

This is very much a book about the power of prices. In the 1870s, economics started striving for the status of a natural science. Before this period, the discipline was often called 'political economy' and it was widely accepted that it was a social science, affected by ideology, philosophy and rampant internal debate. But after this period, it gained a new name and status. Now, it was just known as *economics*. The thinkers of this period desired a physics of society, but they lacked the precise numbers that physics had: kilos, centimetres, volume. They devised an intricate mathematics to solve this problem, and the scientific measure they landed on was *prices*. Price was, and still is, the most exact measure of value in economics. Every aspect of politics today is shaped by this. These numbers sometimes become more real than the lived realities that hide behind them. The price put on something has major implications for whether it is prioritised by the political system. Things that are difficult to fix the price of – care, friends, family, art and rest – live a perilous life in the mathematics of the state.

When everything has a price, a hierarchy is created. At the bottom, we find the things, services and people whose worth is hardest to account for. This doesn't mean that they are actually worthless – just that they are treated by politics and the media as if they are. When something doesn't have a price, its price becomes, by default, zero. The unpriced world is rife with uncertainty.

EXPANDING POWERS

In this book, I focus on economic thinking from Europe and the United States. There's a reason for this. The most powerful economic ideas have spread from these places to nearly every corner of the globe. To participate in the European Union, the United Nations, the World Bank or the International Monetary Fund, you need to follow established economic ideas about the national economy.

The philosopher Olúfẹ́mi O. Táíwò and the historian Michael Franczak have argued that many of the decision-making processes in these organisations are a continuation of colonial history.[21] And then, of course, there is the gentlemen's agreement that the leader of the International Monetary Fund is always European, while the leader of the World Bank is always American.

In order to understand the world, we need to understand how the world's most powerful people think.

In the year 2000, the economist Edward Lazear proudly claimed that economics (as opposed to the other social sciences) was a 'genuine science', and that its methods had 'imperial' power that had 'invaded' territories that had previously been believed unfit for them. I agree with him, but don't know that I would be proud of it.[22]

TO MEASURE IS TO LIVE

Feminism's most important insight is that the people and activities with the highest status in society haven't got there via fair, neutral processes. We always need to take a close look at history to understand why some people and things are praised, while others are put down; why some are paid well, and others poorly. This detective work often uncovers violence, coercion and oppression that has previously been invisible.

The European history of ideas has, understandably, been drawn to the possibility of a discipline that could use rationality to prevent war and conflict, and replace human chaos with apolitical, mathematical and transparent systems. I empathise with this dream; who wouldn't want that? But it created an intense intellectual attraction to everything that could be measured, which meant ignoring or even attempting to eliminate everything in our lives which was unpredictable, embodied and filled with feeling. And that is still the case today.

In the century preceding the Enlightenment, wild things were happening on the European continent. Old ways of living and thinking were being replaced by the new. The witch hunts, enclosure of common lands and violent peasant rebellions all attest to this. At the same time, it was a riveting time for science; a lot of the things we are most proud of today stem from this period. In chapters 1 and 2, I delve into the devastating knock-on effects that the philosophy of this time had for women and care work. Women and the home became black boxes, feared and reviled for their emotionality and unpredictability. Many of the male philosophers of this time denied their own mortality and dependency. They wanted to see themselves as completely independent, so they made the people who cared for them invisible.

In chapter 3, I explore how we built a world where a person's suffering could lead to contempt and ridicule – with Britney Spears lighting our way! Why was she, rather than the paparazzi, managers and gossip bloggers, the target of our ire? The rational individual, *Homo economicus*, who is driven by self-interest, enters the scene, and we will begin to see how the presence of care has become the exception, and the absence of care the norm.

In chapters 4 and 5, I show how economists increased their power and entrenched a new language in politics. The price theory they cooked up was a huge break with what had previously been on the table, with wide-ranging implications for how we value things, even now. Looking at that which has no price, or looking behind a price, has become almost impossible. We will see how economists in the 1900s got closer to politicians and developed the concept of GDP (gross domestic product) – which was a disaster for unpaid care work (and the environment!) because it became valueless both in cultural and monetary terms.

As we move into chapter 6, I discuss how feminism sometimes unintentionally, sometimes with great vigour, has framed men's lives as liberty, and doing care work as oppressive, or even a waste of time. Paid work, we have been told, is real freedom. But for the most vulnerable women, paid work has been a constant part of life – and they do not feel particularly free. I show how we have attempted to keep care cheap at all costs, leading to those who perform it being made out to be both 'naturally' good at it, and unskilled. And I challenge the idea that men's lives are ones women should emulate – after all, how happy do men really seem?

A friend of mine worked at an architecture firm that was bought up by a hedge fund. Her experience and what it meant for the care and joy in her life is recounted in chapter 7. In the workplace, we have come to punish those who care for others, because the value of that work is so difficult to quantify. Only one type of person is optimal: the one who performs on the bottom line, consistently, constantly. Great for the numbers, terrible for people.

Zooming out further and looking at the state, the devaluation of care has led to the use of economic models in policy that have no real grasp on the role that public services play in the economy. In chapters 8 and 9, I track what this has meant for our societies and our lives. Using economic models to optimise and systematise care has turned hospitals into factories and citizens into customers. The care sector is plagued by constant mistrust, criticism and suspicion. Under the guise of rationality and science, a hugely political way to look at what it means to give and receive care has cloaked itself as the only alternative, leading to a massive care crisis that affects us all.

< >

In this book, we're on the trail of a mystery. In 1965, Denmark had a GDP of 750 billion Danish kroner. In

2015, that number was 2,000 billion.[23] The picture is similar all over the world. In 1997 US GDP was $8.58 trillion – while in 2023 it was $27.36 trillion. In the UK, meanwhile, GDP in 1997 was $1.56 trillion; in 2023 it was $3.35 trillion. Why is it that there is so much wealth, yet we feel so terrible? How have we reached a moment where we are at the very pinnacle of monetary and technological progress, but our care systems are crumbling and people are dying on the streets? That is what we must unravel.

I became a feminist because I felt like shit. If I hadn't felt like shit, I would never have become a feminist. When I was 20 years old, I was the victim of digital sexual violence, what we used to call revenge porn. More than anything, I didn't understand what was happening. I didn't understand why other people were treating me the way they did, the shame I felt, and why I didn't get the help and care I so desperately needed. Since then, feminism has helped me understand the world around me. I hope that this book can help you, too, that it can give you a fresh perspective on things that sometimes feel so normalised that you don't even notice them. For me, the work of understanding my society is a way of showing respect for myself and my surroundings. The first order of change is knowing what needs changing. Established economics operates in the shadows, and we need to bring it to light.

People have always said that things couldn't be different. And they have always been wrong.

A MECHANICAL UNIVERSE

'You understood that, for you,
politics was a question of life or death.'

ÉDOUARD LOUIS, *WHO KILLED MY FATHER*

CHAPTER 1

At the end of the 1600s, something changed about the way people related to their surroundings. We call the period that started here and lasted for the next 200 years or so the Enlightenment. What was once dark would now be lit up! Humanity had been drenched in tradition and superstition, but now, scientific methods could be developed based on experiments and empiricism. Mathematics was seen by many as the divine language of the world. Thinkers, scientists and politicians measured and weighed like never before. Order had to be made of the chaos. Early on, the clock became an ideal for the great philosophers. The clock, with its small gears and mechanical functions, was a metaphor for the world. God even became known as the Great Watchmaker. Those who investigated the world saw themselves as the rational ones studying the chaos – and they were, of course, superior to the objects they studied.

It must be said that the Enlightenment was also enormously important in advancing the fight for equal rights for every individual and paving the way for what would eventually become feminism. But the focus on quantification and rationality had serious consequences for the philosophers' ability to understand the meaning of care and human connection. The body was firmly rejected in favour of the mind, and we began to fear things that were unpredictable and emotional.

But even before the Enlightenment, this fear of the body shows up in the work of our greatest thinkers, the ones who still shape the lives we live today. All the way back in antiquity, an irritated Socrates, on his deathbed, dismissed his weeping wife:

> If we are ever to gain untroubled knowledge of anything, we must get rid of [the body], and with the soul by itself look at things in themselves … For if it is impossible to attain to pure knowledge while we are associated with the body, one of two things must follow; either we can nowhere at all acquire it, or only after death … And during our lifetime we shall in this way, I think, make the nearest approach to knowledge, if we abstain as far as possible from intercourse and communication with the body … For that the impure ever attain to the pure is, I fear, unlawful.[1]

In other words: it's better to die than to listen to the body and its needs, and the body is in direct conflict with philosophy and reason. It is precisely this attempt to be superior to the impure, chaotic body and create a 'pure' society that this whole book is about.

Attacks on forms of life that were seen as chaotic intensified in the century leading up to the Enlightenment. When people in the 1500s and 1600s began to think in a more structured way about the state, citizens, work and the economy, animosity began to spread among priests, lords and politicians all over Europe towards the traditional forms of superstition, community and work that were prevalent among peasants. Peasants, who greatly outnumbered everyone else in society, were unruly, lustful and lazy. They rebelled and made trouble. Many of them were killed as a result. And some of them were accused of witchcraft.

In 1486, the *Malleus Maleficarum*, or Hammer of Witches, was written by the German priest Heinrich Kramer and theologist James Sprenger. It was a handbook for identifying witches. The book encouraged its readers to tell priests or judges if they knew, saw or heard 'that any person is reported to be a heretic or witch'.[2] It became a bestseller all over Europe. In Germany alone, there were 16 editions, and in France at least 11 editions by 1700. The *Malleus Maleficarum* wasn't just about witches, but about women's nature in general. Across Europe, priests began to preach about the uncontrollable desire of woman, which was in league with the Devil.[3] The biblical tale about Eve succumbing to temptation in the Garden of Eden, and tempting Adam in turn, served as a constant reminder: woman was cunning; she was duplicitous. Men were encouraged to fear women.[4]

In Germany and Denmark, there were rumours that sleeping with the wrong women might result in having your penis cut off and hidden in a tree. In her book *Caliban and the Witch*, which deals with the relationship between the witch trials and the European economy, the political theorist Silvia Federici writes: 'Certainly we can say that the language of the witch-hunt "produced" the Woman as a different species, a being *sui generis*, more carnal and perverted by nature.'[5]

Men and women who had worked together and shared tasks became estranged from one another. Historians Frances and Joseph Gies write that the woman was the partner of the man: 'often his equal, sometimes more than his equal'. But more and more, women were confined to the tasks associated with children and the home, while the man toiled outside it.[6] This estrangement lives on in modern times in more or less visible ways – for example, in books like John

The myth of penis trees kept by dangerous women was prevalent in various European contexts. These images come from the thirteenth-century French novel, *Le Roman de la Rose*.

Gray's *Men are from Mars, Women are from Venus* (1992), which claims to teach you how to 'understand the opposite sex', as if they spoke another language. Pop culture is full of scheming women who can't be trusted regarding their own desires and intentions. They lie. They manipulate. They bring good men to the brink of insanity with their distortions, like in the song 'What Do You Mean?' by Justin Bieber, when the woman wants to fight, then love, then go to the right, then to the left. She confounds him by nodding, then expressing a wish to say no. In the television series *Mad Men*, the classic Freudian question gets paraphrased when one adman asks: 'What do women want?' and another answers: 'Who cares?'

The woman is an eternal mystery. Can she be trusted? Does she even know what she wants? Can she think logically? A study from 2017 showed that 69 per cent of Europeans believed that women 'were more driven by their emotions' than men.[7] The list goes on.

The historian Maria Mies argued in the 1980s that the witch trials helped create a new kind of state and a new kind of scientific thought. The torture, murders and brutal trials suffered by the accused are often used as an example of the barbarity of the Middle Ages, when in fact, as Mies suggests, they were the first steps toward the new 'political science' that would mark the Enlightenment: a hatred of the supernatural, and a celebration of logic and reason.[8]

Let's not forget that the witch trials were also an economic gold mine for many of the men who were studying law during this time. Those involved in the trials often received money for each person who was convicted and killed, and for overseeing the court proceedings. Cornelius Loos, the first Catholic priest to criticise the witch trials, called it 'a new alchemy, gold and silver coined from human blood'.[9] He was imprisoned for heresy, and in 1592 he was forced to recant his statements.

a mechanical universe > 33

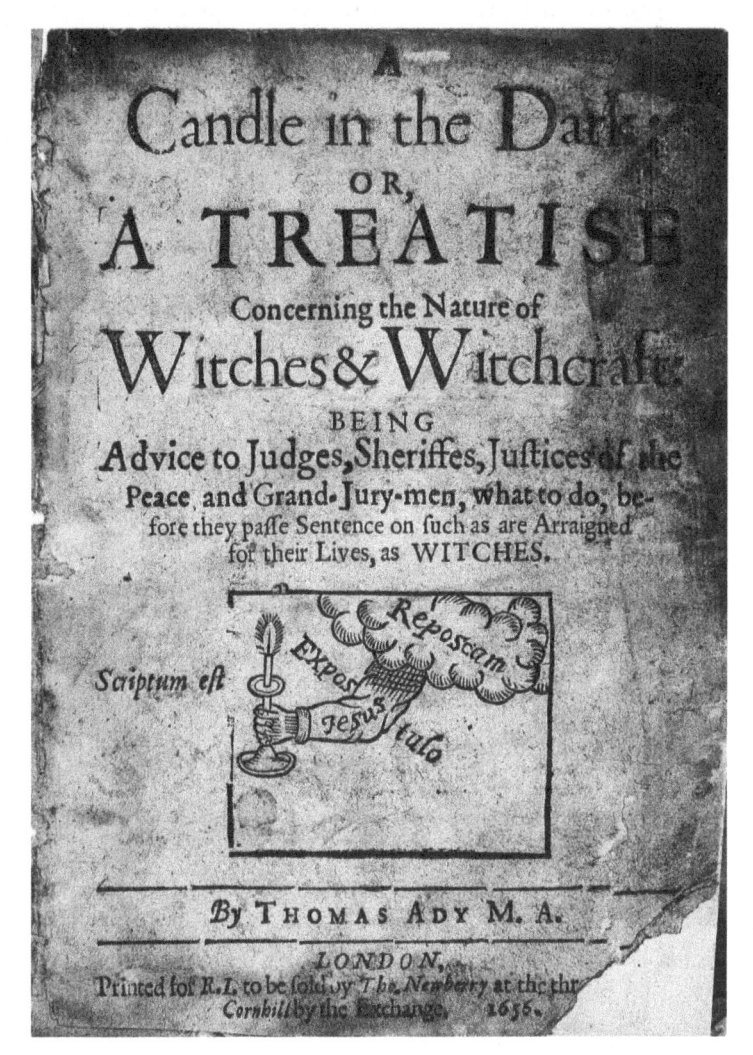

A
Candle in the Dark
OR,
A TREATISE
Concerning the Nature of
Witches & Witchcraft

BEING
Advice to Judges, Sheriffes, Justices of the Peace, and Grand-Jury-men, what to do, before they passe Sentence on such as are Arraigned for their Lives, as WITCHES.

Scriptum est

Reposcam
Expostulo
Jesu

By THOMAS ADY M. A.

LONDON,
Printed for R. I. to be sold by *Tho. Newbery* at the thr...
Cornhill by the Exchange. 1656.

The new light of rationality would be cast upon the witches and reveal them in the eyes of the law. Cover of *A Candle in the Dark*, 1656.

I realise that it's puckish to start a book about the role of economics in our lives with the story of systematic mass murder in the late Middle Ages. But if you want perfect mathematics, you need perfect citizens. If the behaviour of your citizens doesn't fit the ideal, they need to be put in their place. And there was, as we shall see, a clear link between the prevailing economic theory of the time and the citizens who had to be eliminated.

NEW WORKERS, NEW TIMES

The political thinker Jean Bodin resided in France in the 1500s. He saw himself as a vanguard of the new rational way of thinking, and he wrote about the role of the state in the enlightened society that was to come. If you encounter Bodin today, it will likely be in the form of praise for his work on the economic theory called mercantilism, or as one of the first thinkers to write at length about the causes of inflation.

Mercantalism emphasised the importance of exports but also believed that the more people that lived in a country, the richer that country would be. The more the merrier! For that reason, he was keenly interested in the family and the role women played in the production of new workers. There was an extreme labour shortage in

Europe, which concerned many in the higher ranks of society. Who would till their fields?

In 1580, Bodin published his book *De la démonomanie des sorciers* (On the Demon-mania of Witches). In it, he wrote that women were selfish pleasure seekers who took all too lightly their duty to the state of creating new workers. He suggested that a special police force should be created to monitor midwives and witches, who he claimed were responsible for abortions, sex without conception as well as infertility – and were therefore guilty of abetting women in neglecting their true responsibility to society. He knew that many of those accused of witchcraft were beloved and respected for their medical knowledge among their local communities, but – lest one be duped! – he wrote: 'for evil spirits never do good, except by accident or in order that a greater evil might come of it, when for example they cure a sick person to attract him to their devotion.'[10] Even when these women did good things, it was always with an ulterior motive. 'What does it mean?' Jean Bodin wondered, when a woman is loved by her community and cures them of maladies? That she's a witch, of course! The book was extremely popular, getting reprinted ten times, and it was translated into both German and Latin. It contained detailed instructions for how to suspend the legal system's usual processes to punish witches even more harshly than other criminals.

In *Caliban and the Witch*, Silvia Federici describes how the new and more systematic state order sought to deprive women of their knowledge of their own bodies as well as the little freedom they had. Eliminating sex for pleasure or outside of marriage was deemed crucial. Jean Bodin worked as an adviser to the French state on the persecution of witches and was a proponent of torture. At this point in history, convicted witches were subject to extremely violent forms of torture. Entire populations could be disciplined by being forced to watch the violence enacted on the undesirable elements of society. Bodin wrote: 'Now, if there is any means to appease the wrath of God, to gain his blessing, to strike awe into some by the punishment of others, to preserve some from being infected by others, to diminish the number of evil-doers, to make secure the life of the well-disposed, and to punish the most detestable crimes of which the human mind can conceive, it is to punish with the utmost rigor the witches.'

Bodin's overt bloodlust has led some historians to write that there were two Bodins: a political genius who laid the foundations of the modern state through the systematic measurement of citizens, and a madman who hunted witches. But Bodin's focus on population growth and his witch hunts were intrinsically connected.[11] The control of labour was one of Bodin's rational ideals. He hunted witches because they prevented pregnancies and therefore the production of new labour. According to mercantilism, which was the established economics of the time, they were an obstacle to prosperity. In mercantilism, citizens were a means to increase 'the prosperity of merchants, manufacturers and financiers', writes historian Johannes Overbeek.[12] That might feel familiar.

The historians Gunnar Heinsohn and Otto Steiger have argued that it is impossible to separate Bodin's witch-hunting from his rationality. In the 1990s, they wrote that Bodin prioritised the production of a new child and future worker over the mother's survival. 'Therefore,' they conclude, 'Bodin, the economist, cannot be regarded as a universal genius if Bodin, the demonologist, is regarded as an irrational fool.'[13]

We have a tendency to talk about culture on the one hand and economics on the other. But what we learn from the witch trials is that economic theories shape our culture and determine which forms of life are seen as the *right* ones. Social norms and women's status are connected to the roles they play in the economy.

The wild, lazy, hedonistic peasants (of all genders!), who enjoyed life, had sex for fun and didn't want to work all the time – either in the home or outside of it – were straightened out because of economic theories about how they could create the most value.

Systematic thinking required mechanical and predictable behaviour. In order for Bodin to measure, he needed to make the lives of individual people easier to deal with: more similar, more structured and more submissive to the authorities. The new social order required the taming of the wild elements. What you want to measure shapes what you want to have.

A CONTROLLABLE WORLD

The witch trials were part of a larger cultural movement that marked the transition towards a more enlightened future. Witches were associated with backwards forms of life, while the methods used to capture, investigate, torture and convict them were seen as new.[14] The Enlightenment, which followed soon after, became a reckoning with the power of superstition and the backdrop for scientific breakthroughs, which these new theories about the state and money were part of.[15] Now God's clock will be opened! The economist Julie Nelson writes: 'the predominant cultural conception of the relationship between humans and nature changed from one in which humans were seen as embedded in a female, living cosmos to one in which men were seen as potentially detached, objective observers and controllers of nature. In this new conception, nature came to be seen as passive and, eventually, as mechanical.'[16]

Here we find a paradox that will follow us throughout these pages. Nature is mechanical, but it is also uncontrollable and dangerous. It needs to be *observed and measured*, so that it can be mastered. From the start, the Enlightenment thinkers were frustrated that, while they believed that humans and nature were mechanical, it seemed that most people didn't actually want to behave in a systematic way. Many of the peasants who were supposed to be systematised and optimised to maximise gains, for example, would rather take a nap than work. During these years, there were constant peasant riots across Europe because peasants believed they were being worked too hard and didn't have enough free time.

What is the heart, as the philosopher Thomas Hobbes (who we'll be hearing more about soon) wrote in *Leviathan* (1651), 'but a spring; and the nerves, but so many strings; and the joints, but so many wheels, giving motion to the whole body.'[17] But if the heart was merely a spring, why didn't the peasant work like a machine? What kind of wheels and springs riot?

The concept of a mechanical body kept recurring, despite the peasants' fight for a nap. The French philosopher René Descartes (1596–1650) divided the world into *res cogitans*, the soul or mind that thinks, and *res extensa*, that which is material or natural. Descartes took Socrates' ideas about the pure soul and the sinful body to the next level. *Res extensa* was completely cut off from the consciousness and the soul, and represented our baser drives: 'I desire, I say, that you should consider that these functions follow in this machine simply from the disposition of the organs as wholly naturally as the movements of a clock or other automaton follow from the disposition of its counterweights and wheels.'[18] *Res extensa*, the physical body, is permeated by a now familiar contradiction: the body contains desire and feelings, but it is also, according to these thinkers, mechanical. This contradiction shapes many of the problems that economics continues to struggle with today.

In Descartes' understanding, the body was mechanical. When we touched fire, for example, a message would be sent to our brain, which would release a liquid that would make the muscles contract. The feelings of the mind were divorced from the body. Illustration from *Traité de l'Homme*, 1664.

UNRULY LADIES

The dream of being able to predict and reduce the world to mathematics met its first great match in the Enlightenment thinkers' encounter with their own chaotic insides. The historian Liz Fee describes the early Enlightenment philosophers' views of women: 'The woman gives [the rational man] a connection to nature, reminds him of childhood, reminds him of the body, reminds him of sexuality, passion and human relationships. She is the container of all the emotional and all the irrational parts of being human.'[19] In the satirical pamphlet *The Parliament of Women* from 1646, women in politics are represented as the ultimate image of anarchy. The joke of the piece is that if women had influence they would establish a society with 'more Ease, Pompe, Pride, and wantonnesse.'[20] A society that listens to the needs of the body is illogical, dangerous, and decidedly ridiculous. The philosophers felt that women were uncontrollable because they stirred uncontrollable and difficult feelings in themselves.[21]

With the rise of a more organised study of medicine, many women were sidelined in fields they had previously dominated. Women were excluded and demoted in the field of midwifery, for instance. In 1733, Edmund Chapman, a male midwife, wrote in his book *A Treatise*

THE Parliament of VVomen.

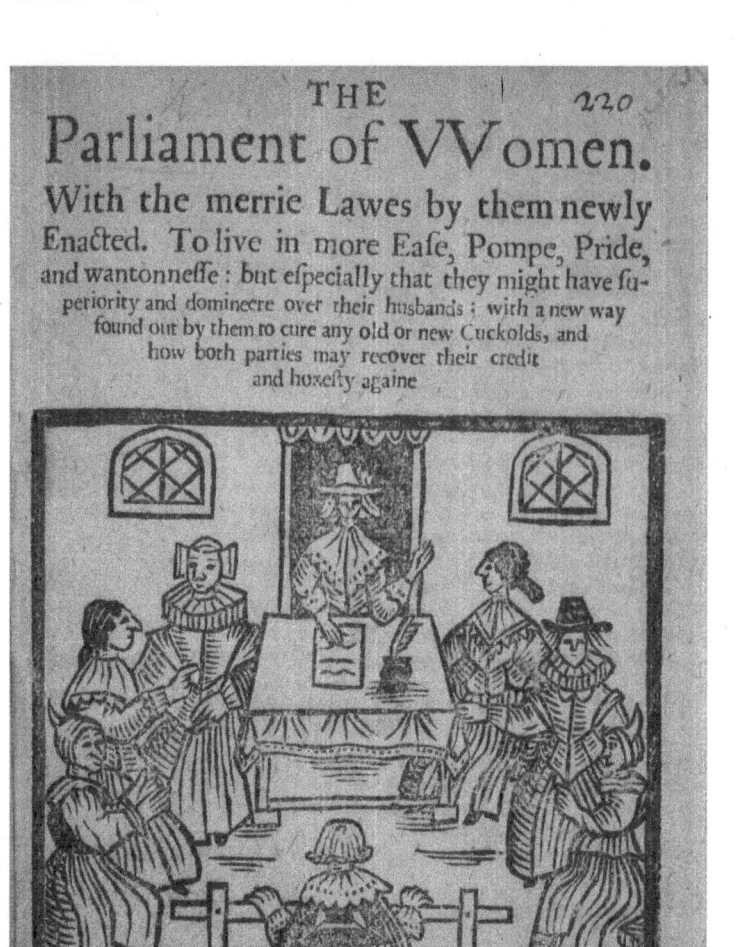

With the merrie Lawes by them newly Enacted. To live in more Eafe, Pompe, Pride, and wantonneffe: but efpecially that they might have fuperiority and domineere over their husbands; with a new way found out by them to cure any old or new Cuckolds, and how both parties may recover their credit and honefty againe

London, Printed for *W. Wilfon* and are to be fold by him in *Will yard* in Little Saint *Bartholomewes*. 1646.

The Parliament of Women was a satirical pamphlet clearly amping up the connection between women, emotions and lack of discipline. If women were in power, they would fight for dangerous things like 'ease', 'pompe' and 'wantonnesse'.

on the Improvement of Midwifery, that women may attend and provide assistance during deliveries, but that if there arose a need for medical instruments, then she should without delay call on a man of character and expertise.[22] Elizabeth Nihell, a female midwife, rebelled against the exclusion of women from midwifery as a result of the new scientific approach to their domain. In 1760, she wrote in *A Treatise on the Art of Midwifery* that, in her experience, men did not have sufficient patience and were hasty to intervene, heightening the risk of death or injury for both the child and the mother. And, she writes, they 'prostitute [meaning abuse, in this context] women's bodies' for science, without caring about the process of childbirth or women's physical and emotional well-being.[23] Nihell saw a clear link between the new way of thinking about science and the inability to understand the human and emotional connections that carers needed to have with their patients. She did not believe that childbirth was mechanical.

More recently, the historian Lisa Forman Cody has described how early male midwives believed that women had too much passion and sympathy for the pregnant women to exercise the rationality required to assist them. Rationality was defined as an absence of empathy, and medical instruments were often used to tug the child through the birth canal and thereby to take control over the slowness of nature, whereas female midwives, according to Nihell, would rather wait and see. Nihell was later called 'a lunatic, not lucid ... [who] sets up her throat ... with the fluency of a fish-woman' by a male midwife.[24]

The example of midwifery is important for understanding this time period. While rapid and significant scientific developments were made in the field, saving many, many lives in the process, the new male midwives began to see pregnant women differently.[25] The person practising medicine and the person receiving medical care were no longer equals. The person practising medicine had power over the patient. Women were, according to another male midwife, John Leake, driven by their hearts rather than their brains, because when one had an emotional connection to childbirth (because of having experienced it, for example), one could not be impartial.[26] Concrete experience was disqualified in favour of scientific observation. The unfeeling observer was the only one who could see the situation clearly. As the male midwife Louis Lapeyre wrote in 1772: 'a midwife is like an animal who has nothing of the woman left, but the weakness of her understanding, the wretched prejudices of old doting women'.[27]

Obviously, these scientists helped to make critical advances in medicine. But the branding of emotional relationships as unscientific *and therefore inferior* has had an unbelievable impact on Western culture. The new medical practitioners tried to take emotion out of human interactions, rendering them cold, quantifiable, and supposedly effective instead. This has shaped which kinds of knowledge are considered true and medically legitimate. And this change didn't only affect women, but all of us. We are only now learning how intertwined our bodies and minds actually are.[28]

The parts of society that lived up to these mechanical ideals were praised while the parts that didn't were hidden away, above all the body's functions and feelings. The American clergyman Cotton Mather could barely hide his disgust at having a body when, in the 1680s, he wrote about what a dreadful humiliation it was to have to urinate: 'What mean, and vile Things are the Children of Men, in this mortal State! How much do our *natural Necessities* abase us, and place us in some regard, on the same Level with the very *Dogs*! ... Accordingly, I resolved, that it should be my ordinary Practice, whenever I step to answer the one or other Necessity of Nature, to make it an Opportunity of shaping in my Mind, some holy, noble, divine Thought.'[29] It was precisely in this bodily sphere – the sphere of dogs! – that women took care of bodies and minds. They spent time dealing with what couldn't be managed, on what couldn't be measured. It was frightening. And these men were right in some respects. It is pretty terrifying to have another human depend on you, or to deal with your body when it gets sick without warning. Nothing is as fluid and unpredictable as a relationship of care. When we need other people, when we listen to our body and our feelings, we inhabit a space that we never have full control over. These enlightened thinkers didn't want to think about that.[30]

The historian Eduard Jan Dijksterhuis sums up the massive consequences of the mechanical world view in his iconic book, *The Mechanization of the World Picture* (1961): 'It is a historical fact that it has had deep and far-reaching consequences for all of society that we have embraced the mechanical way of seeing the world ... some praise it as a symptom of the gradual sharpening of human intellect ... others see it, while also recognizing its importance for progress, theoretical understanding and the practical control of nature, as no less than a catastrophic influence on philosophy, science and society.'[31] This is a paradox that runs through the entire history of economics. What happens to everything that isn't mechanical when you use mechanical tools and theories to describe the world?

Many of the men who retreated from the body were rich and had people to take care of them, while they desperately denied that they ever pissed. It is the lives of their employees we must turn to if we want a fuller picture of what it means to be fully human.

In 1739, Mary Collier wrote a collection of poetry called *The Woman's Labour*. She worked as a washerwoman, and in the poems she describes her doings and work days:

> *When Ev'ning does approach, we homeward hi*
> *And our domestick Toils incessant ply:*
> *Against your coming Home prepare to get*
> *Our Work all don, Our House in order set;*
> *Bacon and Dumpling in the Pots we boil,*
> *Our Beds we make, our Swine we feed the while;*
> *And set the Table out against you come:*
> *Early next Morning owe on you attend,*
> *Our tender Babes unto the Field we bear*
> *And wrap them in our Cloaths to keep them warm,*
> *While round about we gather up the Corn;*[32]

Collier shows us how life consists of the work of taking care of pigs and the house and carrying children – Our tender Babes – while plodding through the fields. What moves me most is her sense of connection to all that she writes about. The approaching evening, the bacon in the pot, making the beds, the baby close to her body in its sling, harvesting the crops. No person can be isolated from another. Everything that we do has something to do with other people. Caring for a child, preparing dinner, and communing with the nature that will soon become food – it is all interconnected.

Collier's poem gets to the core of feminist economics. She knows that what happens in the home is work. That it takes time and effort, that it both confines us *and* creates value for society and the person performing the labour. Bundling up a child is work. But it is also love. Bundling up a child takes time from paid work. But it also creates a new human.

The early economic thinkers had to discount this doubleness to create a precise, mathematical system to describe production, exchange and value. But the market cannot be isolated from the rest of life – it is part of everything that we are and do.

WHO GETS TO BE FREE?

'I'll tell you what freedom is to me. No fear.'
NINA SIMONE

CHAPTER 2

As we have now established, a mechanical world view requires its individual cogs and components to behave systematically and predictably. They must also be relatively alike. The good thing about 1 + 1 = 2 is that two identical ones make two. Even when we write 1 + 3 = 4, a one is still a one. The one doesn't change because it is added to a three. It is solid and distinct. As the study of economics began to take shape during the Enlightenment, it quickly became clear that one of its foremost tasks was to figure out what traits all people shared. If the economists could figure that one out, every one of us could be studied like gears in the machine. But it was clear from the start that it was going to be pretty difficult, because people affected each other and changed over the course of their lives.

One of the first philosophers of the economic project was the Englishman Thomas Hobbes. Hobbes' masterpiece, the aforementioned *Leviathan*, was published in 1651, and its influence has been enormous.

Inspired by the scientist Galileo Galilei, Hobbes was convinced that it was possible to make a system that could describe all of human behaviour. Galilei was known for saying that the universe was a book written in the language of mathematics. Since God had created such stable natural laws, he must also have created stable laws of human behaviour. Hobbes' dedication to mathematics knew no bounds. He even speculated that our thoughts and decisions were a result of an inner mathematics.

In his book *De Corpore* (1655), he writes: 'By *ratiocination* [or reasoning], I mean *computation*. Now to compute, is either to collect the sum of many things that are added together, or to know what remains when one thing is taken out of another. *Ratiocination*, therefore, is the same with *addition* and *substruction*.'[1] That might seem overly clinical, but it is still how established economics often thinks. Thinking in mathematic terms meant being an enlightened, dignified human. And in many ways, this was a major step forward; many philosophers now believed that the 'right' form of thinking could be achieved across socio-economic classes, whereas many had previously insisted that only upper-class men were capable of making informed decisions. But this also meant that those people deemed unmathematical, illogical and irrational were condemned as unenlightened and unworthy.

Hobbes' best-known theory is about the state of nature. It describes who he believes we are without culture, religion, social norms or political order. Hobbes hypothesised that we were fundamentally driven by a desire for dominance, a need to conquer our fellow human beings. He argued that if human beings were not governed by a head of state, we would descend into endless wars and a 'solitary, poor, nasty, brutish and short' life, as he put it. Deep down in mankind was a drive, and it wasn't pretty. If ethics and morals weren't forced down our throats, we would be chopping off each other's heads before long.

Hobbes had a great deal of trouble including families in his theory, and he didn't say much more on the subject other than that the father was the king of the house and everyone else his subject, and that it was undeniable that people tended to want to get laid. Hobbes was interested in the individual, and he did not spend much time reflecting on the warm feelings individuals had for others. To get around the obvious challenges present in a theory of humanity absent a single coherent thought about the family, he wrote that his philosophy should be read as a thought experiment, in which people 'had just emerged from the earth like mushrooms and grown up without any obligation to each other'.[2] In other words: *please*, don't worry about childbirth, breastfeeding, learning to speak or walk, and other minor things like that.

Here, we find a strategy we will encounter again and again: creating a hypothetical assumption to make the world fit the theory. Economic history is rife with hypothetical humans and scenarios. In order to portray society as mechanical, Hobbes dismissed everything that didn't fit his theory. Hobbes eliminated childhood and care so that he wouldn't have to admit that people are not always competing with one another. In reality, people *often* look after each other.[3]

I get his dilemma, to a certain extent. Hobbes wanted to prove that everyone was essentially equal, but in order to do so he erased the fact that some people are born sick, that some have living parents and others don't, that some can walk and others can't, that some are rich and others are poor. Sameness became the necessary condition for a theory of equality. A theory in which people neither need to provide nor receive care to live.

It is quite the philosophical acrobatics trick to ignore the existence of childbirth and replace it with chanterelles. And people noticed even back then. In 1704, the philosopher Mary Astell had a jab at Hobbes: 'How I lament my Stars that it was not my good Fortune to Live in those Happy Days when Men sprung up like so many Mushrooms ... without Father or Mother or any sort of dependency!'⁴ Astell reveals a fairly central problem in Hobbes' thinking – not only the omission of childbirth, but also people's dependence on one another to survive. In Hobbes' view, the freest human – the human who will lead us into Enlightenment – does not depend on anyone. Instead we are served an autodidactic, power-hungry mushroom.

Mary Astell has largely been written out of the history of Western thought, despite being quite a powerhouse in her time. A new Danish translation of Hobbes was published in 2020.

FREEDOM FROM ONE ANOTHER

In the years after Hobbes' *Leviathan*, a debate raged in England about the best way to lead a state. The victor was the British philosopher and first real 'political scientist' John Locke, who established his liberal perspective in his *Two Treatises of Government*, the first of which was published in 1689.

In the first treatise, Locke decreed a new, democratic order: all men were created equal, had the right to participate in democracy, to own and sell their labour and keep for themselves whatever they chose to spend their money on. It was the task of the state to protect these rights. People should no longer inherit power and influence, they should achieve it by merit. Obviously, these are all good ideas that we are still struggling to realise.

But they also meant that, for Locke, a millionaire or a street sweeper were essentially equal because they were logical, rational and could participate in a democracy. Locke also believed women were capable of rational thought, and – unlike many others in his time – had the right to an education.[5]

Even though Locke acknowledged that inequality existed among men and women (the stronger men could work harder and earn more money) and between employers and employees (because employers were often richer), he nonetheless argued that marriage and working relationships were freely entered into, no matter how unequal the parties involved. This world view came to be known as contract theory, in which society was seen as a series of contracts that were voluntarily made between free people. The position from which one entered a contract was not so important. Locke created the foundation for the role the state plays in our lives today.

Locke made a distinction between what happens in the home and what happens outside of it. Outside the walls of the home, strength should not matter. Everyone was equal. But in the home, he felt it made sense that men had more influence because they were stronger. Curious! Locke, like Hobbes, struggled to reconcile the domestic sphere with his ambitious theories of ownership and individual freedom. To circumvent this, he claimed that work that took place in the home was God-given, rather than human work, and was therefore not productive or related to the economy. Apparently, God was the one making and raising the kids.[6]

For Locke, the home, which was primarily the domain of women, was a spiritual, Christian sphere, detached from state, political and economic concerns. There would always be care in the world because it came from God, who had created the world. On the other hand, men and their wives owned the work of servants in their homes. How exactly can one support individual freedom and the right to own the fruits of your labour, yet not believe that the people who work in people's homes have the same rights?

Paradoxes like these are typical of Enlightenment thinking about the home and what happens there. The philosophers wanted to show that mathematics, man and the market were natural extensions of one another, but they kept stumbling over housework, love, family and children. What the hell is a household? A company? All about sex? A contract? Love? So far, we've got mushrooms and God as workarounds.

By contrast, the French philosopher François Poulain de la Barre, in 1673, 16 years before Locke's magnum opus, wondered why 'We offer great rewards to a man who can tame a tiger, admire those who can train horses, monkeys, and elephants, and praise to the skies the author of some modest work. Yet we neglect women who have spent years and years nourishing and educating children.'[7] There have always been people who have recognised the value of the work of being there for others.

As the economist Nancy Folbre shows in *Greed, Lust and Gender*, the home was left out of political theory.[8] This spared Locke a fair number of complicated questions, as it did Hobbes. It is easier to define freedom when you are talking about people with adult bodies and minds, who are capable of working and earning money, who are not impelled to look after others and never feel forced to do anything but serve their own interests. Political theory's leading man is a fictional character.

Locke paints a picture of a free, independent, isolated person. But his understanding of freedom rests on a secret: this freedom is only possible for some because it is denied to others, particularly women and servants. Along with Hobbes, Locke created a definition of freedom that is only available to those who live at the expense of others. Freedom is a life in which others set you free by invisibly meeting your needs, so that you are able to exist as pure mind, which is the human ideal. Basic physical and emotional needs were stashed away in the home, shameful, taboo and irrational.[9]

STRONG, SELF-RELIANT AND NAÏVE

Most of us have experienced the shame that comes with realising and articulating that you need other people. When I experienced digital sexual violence in 2011, I didn't ask for help. I thought that strong people had to be in full control, that they managed everything on their own. Help was for weak people. If you had to ask for it, you probably didn't deserve it. That might sound extreme, but taking Western philosophy into consideration, that gut feeling makes perfect sense. When I became an activist for victims of sexual violence, advocating for things like free counselling and aiming to broaden people's understanding of the issue, I repeatedly heard that I was demanding too much from other people. No one owed me respect.

And I felt ashamed. I was ashamed of being so miserable and so desperately needing help. I thought that everyone else was getting by just fine on their own, so I didn't think that I had any right to help. What I didn't realise, of course, was that by virtue of my upbringing, my skin colour, my sexuality and my education, society had taken care of me for my entire life. I only realised that I had been a fish, swimming in care, when suddenly I was on dry land all on my own.

Many people will still to this day deny that they are dependent on the emotional care of others to be happy. But even in 1922, the pioneering American sociologist Charles Horton Cooley wrote: 'Many people of balanced mind and congenial activity scarcely know that they care what others think of them, and will deny [it], perhaps with indignation ... But this is illusion. If failure or disgrace arrives ... he will perceive from the shock, the fear, the sense of being outcast and helpless, that he was living in the minds of others without knowing it, just as we daily walk the solid ground without thinking how it bears us up.'[10] In recent years an avalanche of research has shown how important respect is for our well-being, not only mentally, but also physically. In 2015, a team of Canadian researchers discovered that twice as many instances of ulcerative colitis – the sickness I have – occurs among people who had been exposed to sexual violence as children.[11]

< >

Locke's ideal society, in which freedom means escaping the responsibilities of physical and psychological care, would not function in reality. The early political thinkers put forth a universal ideal, which by definition was never going to be accessible to everyone. Certain people *must* provide care to others at the cost of their personal time. The question is who, and under what circumstances?

The shortcomings of Locke's simplified understanding of freedom are glaringly obvious when it comes to parenthood. What is freedom when a person will die if you don't pick them up, make them breakfast or make sure they don't run off a cliff? Their body is yours, and your body is theirs. Their time is yours, and your time is theirs. What would it mean to 'do as you please'?

But the limits of Locke's theory are apparent elsewhere, too. They are visible anytime we negotiate between our own desires and the needs of others. When our culture does not adequately address that we don't all have the same baseline for entering 'contracts', nor that we are all dependent on each other's respect and care, much is left in the shadows. The South African writer Sisonke Msimang writes that mothers with children who are vulnerable because of their skin colour or social status not only have to deal with their own rage at their loss of 'freedom' in motherhood, but must also convey to their children that the freedom they've been deluded into believing exists out in the world is an illusion.[12] Because they cannot take social care for granted. Locke teaches us that hard work leads to success, and that everyone should be treated equally. A nice thought. But there is no evidence of it being the current state of affairs. It is an idealistic simplification. And for that reason, his theory was well suited to mathematics.

HOBBES AND LOCKE LAY THE FOUNDATIONS

Many of the assumptions made by Locke became central to the unfolding of economic theory. The first was his concept of freedom: the right to sell one's labour and keep the money one has earned. In this theory, the money that you earn is a reflection of the value you have created, and it follows that it is just that you get to keep it. Therefore, the state must protect private property.

The second order of Enlightenment business was freedom of expression and the right to participate in democracy. In a famous essay, the liberal philosopher Isaiah Berlin distinguishes between negative and positive rights. Negative rights were the ones Locke was interested in, and that constitutions all over the world continue to be based on. For Berlin, negative rights are those which remove obstacles to 'self-realization'.[13]

These are the rights that grant you the freedom from having to do anything for other people.[14]

Positive rights, however, are the rights to receive something involving others – education for instance, or medical treatment when you're sick. You can think about negative rights as the right to be free *from* something and positive rights as the right *to* something. For the early political theorists, negative rights were the only ones the state should protect. Apparently, people could exist without having taken hours and hours of somebody else's 'freedom'. In this framework, it becomes impossible to acknowledge that income, speech or democratic participation are always a direct consequence of the care of others.

In other words, we lose the political language for our interdependence. The fear of the body and of the loss of control that is part and parcel of human life is written into the definition of the state, and becomes invisible. As the philosopher Seyla Benhabib writes, this understanding of the role of the state implies that, 'The law reduces insecurity, the fear of being engulfed by the other, by defining mine and thine … as long as each can keep what is his and attain more by fair rules of the game, he is entitled to it … The law contains anxiety by defining rigidly the boundaries between self and other … but the … anxiety that the other is always looking to interfere in your space and appropriate what is yours ... remains.'[15]

The ultimate fear is that you will have to live your life for another as your mother has lived her life for you. That someone will take up your time, and deprive you of the right to do or say exactly as you please at any given time.

The boundary between oneself and another is of the utmost importance – this is mine, and this is yours – and there is nothing like care to erase that boundary between mine and yours. And this erasure becomes the most dangerous thing of all. These thinkers wanted to be taken care of, but they didn't want to be forced to take care of anyone else. So, they made the care they themselves received invisible in politics.

What is essential here is not necessarily the things that the early political economists said about women. Rather, it is the omission of the 'unfree' life that women come to *symbolise* that has major implications for Western thought and economic theory. The life of a woman was, for early political economists, humiliating. The struggle for freedom was always for the right to avoid receiving or providing care, never for the right to give or receive it. The people we need most are those we are most frightened of becoming. They are looked down on, even though they keep us alive.

They remind us of our own needs, our bodily limits, our profound dependence on one another.

And to this day, we look down on the 'nagging' mother, who makes you eat your vegetables, the 'unambitious' public employee, who wastes away among the elderly and the sick for meagre pay, and the 'office mum', who stays in the same job until retirement and knows the names of everyone's children. All these people keep us healthy, happy and alive. But we don't aspire to become them. We have been taught that people like this do not propel society forward. *We can't live with them, we can't live without them.*

I have great respect for Hobbes and Locke, and it is important to consider them in their historical context. The idea that every human is inviolable, and that we all have the same rights, on paper, to take part in the market and participate in democracy on an equal footing is so essential. Their thinking made a huge difference, and still does, regardless of your gender. There probably wouldn't be any feminism without Hobbes and Locke.

But their inability to recognise that not everyone has the same starting point or the same responsibilities creates problems when their theories are used in political practice. And they are both still enormously popular. When a person calls themselves a 'classic liberal', you're usually dealing with a fan of Locke.

Their theories sound great on paper: everyone is equal regardless of their gender, skin colour, ethnicity, religion, and they should compete on the same turf, and if you win on this turf, you will get the spoils that belong to you. But that was a dream. And sometimes dreams become theories, but that doesn't make them real.

Of course, one should be free to 'do what one wants' within the bounds of the law. But in reality, this does not bring us much closer to understanding our day-to-day lives. We are not isolated mushrooms – we constantly depend on one another and have obligations to one another. It is easy to make fun of Hobbesian fungi, but Locke has the same problem. He describes a world in which freedom means never being forced to do anything. But he doesn't describe any of the needs that are part of human life: being looked after when ill, receiving respect, love and recognition, performing child rearing or education. The mere fact of our existence compels other people to do things for us. Every single person's existence requires other people to be there for them. This is an essential part of human life. But these basic necessities were omitted in favour of an understanding of freedom that was defined as freedom from other people. And as wonderful as that might sound, it is wholly contrived. There are no freedoms

– freedom of speech, freedom of assembly, the right to own property – that can be realised without other people taking care of you.

P.S. Mushrooms actually do care for each other. They communicate and share nourishment if any of them are struggling to survive. Mushrooms can flirt and be rejected. Mushrooms are social beings.[16]

THROUGH THE EYE OF A NEEDLE

'SHEAR MADNESS: Bald Britney a buzz kill'

NEW YORK POST, 19 FEBRUARY 2007

CHAPTER 3

through the eye of a needle > 71

●

In 2007, the singer Britney Spears shaved her hair off in Tarzana, California, and a few days later she hit a paparazzo with an umbrella. The whole world was watching, aghast. Here was a woman who had lost her mind. I was 16 and remember being convinced that she was going to die by suicide. Everyone was talking about it, and it was on the national news. In the end, Spears was forcibly placed under a conservatorship. She lost the right to vote and have a bank account and she lost custody of her children. She became a child in the eyes of the law. The drama surrounding Spears and our reaction to her tells us something important about the consequences of the social theories of the Enlightenment thinkers – consequences they couldn't have foreseen. The Enlightenment thinkers helped to create the ideal of the rational human being. But in so doing, they created the rational human's antithesis: the madwoman.

Spears' conservatorship lasted for 13 years.

< >

The father of modern economics is the Scottish moral philosopher Adam Smith (1723–90). He is the greatest thinker in the field of what we call classical economics. He described the economic structure that arose in 1700s England. From 1700 to 1800, London's population doubled. Hordes of people moved not only from country to city, but also from one way of living and working to another. Many of those who ended up working in the industrialised factories came from families who had been peasants or craftsmen in their local villages.

Large tracts of land, which the peasants had previously shared with each other – called commons – were enclosed by lords and barons, so that large-scale crop farming could be implemented and optimised. This meant that most ordinary people could no longer support themselves outside of dense cities. Paid work became the primary form of employment for those who didn't own land or machines and weren't from rich families. Many more people started working for a boss who made a profit from their labour.

Smith's economic masterpiece is the *The Wealth of Nations* (1776). In the famous economist Max Lerner's introduction to the book in a 1937 edition, he writes: 'It has done as much perhaps as any modern book thus far to shape the whole landscape of life as we live it today.'[1] Adam Smith didn't just describe the changes he saw. He explained them so clearly that they came to be seen as an inevitable expression of human nature.

His was a gargantuan book with a lot to say. But the theory that has had the greatest influence on established economics today is his theory of the division of labour – what we would now call a sort of assembly line. It doesn't take a genius to see why a historical period that was obsessed with mechanical machines and clocks would swoon over the efficiency of the factory.

In most small towns, a single man had been responsible for making needles, and he made as many needles as the townspeople required. But no longer. Now, in the factory, labour could be divided so that multiple people could repeat their respective parts of the production process all through the working day. One person gathered the raw material, one sharpened, one made a hole, one polished, and so on, with up to 18 different people doing separate tasks. Adam Smith was obsessed with this type of process. And so, the theory of the wealth creation of the factory was born. With the division of labour, many, many more needles could be made than ever before. In fact, more needles could be made than we'd ever require! And because it was easier, faster and cheaper to make them, they could be sold for a higher price than it cost to make them. So there was greater productivity and a greater chance of making a profit. Workers, machines, assembly lines, products. The human being and the factory become one.

According to Adam Smith, this is how value is created in the economy: by selling products on the market that are made as efficiently as possible from available resources. If you love detailed descriptions, then Smith's book has plenty to offer, but I won't go into them here. What I'm interested in is everything that Smith *left out*.

Adam Smith wasn't the only one who found needle factories very, very, very interesting. This illustration is from the *Encyclopédie* edited by Denis Diderot and Jean le Rond d'Alembert, 1751–72, and depicts the various parts of the production process.

Smith reinforced the divide we've seen in the work of earlier theorists between everything public, value-creating, and systematic on the one hand and everything private, valueless, and emotional on the other.

Reading *The Wealth of Nations*, you might be led to believe that women hardly exist or do anything economical at all. Smith mentions a few women who knit or work with textiles. But the book's primary legacy is the clear division between the home, in which 'empathetic' and 'impulsive' women create the family with their husbands, and the actual economic sphere outside the home, where politics and trade take place.[2] There is nothing in the book about the creation of the workforce. Smith just off-handedly states that the supply of children born will follow the demand.[3] Adult, able bodies stand at the ready outside the factory. The economist Sumitra Shah describes the role of women in Smith's thinking: 'Women were now to be consumers and transmitters of cultural norms, to the exclusion of any productive responsibility.'[4] The notion that what happened in the family could create economic value was completely absent. In fact, just as with Locke, the home and the maintenance of people's well-being was not seen as the concern of political economics.

THE MOTHER OF ECONOMICS

In *The Wealth of Nations*, Smith takes Hobbes' mechanical mushroom to the next level by arguing that the market is propelled forward by self-interest. In one of his most famous quotes, Smith reflects on what drives us when we work and trade: 'It is not from the benevolence of the butcher, the brewer or the baker that we expect our dinner, but from their regard to their own interest. We address ourselves, not to their humanity, but to their self-love, and never talk to them of our own necessities, but of their advantages. Nobody but a beggar chooses to depend chiefly upon the benevolence of his fellow-citizens.'[5]

We often call the man described here *Homo economicus*, or the economic man. When a man makes a decision, he is making a calculation, and all men make decisions based on their own interest in expanding their property. Self-interest is the driving force of a mechanical market.

There is a lot to unpack here, but for a start: Adam Smith's dinners were not made by male butchers or bakers. As Katrine Marçal recounts in her memorable book *Who Cooked Adam Smith's Dinner?*, Smith enjoyed the 'benevolence' of his mother, Margaret Douglas, and later his cousin, Janet Douglas. These women cooked his meals, did his laundry and cleaned up after him so that Smith could write and teach. But even so, Smith never saw himself as a beggar! He took for granted that there would always be people in society who are not exclusively driven by their own interests, but spend a large amount of their lives serving the self-interest of others. People like his mother.

But despite this, self-interest was still a law of nature present in all people and the entire economic system. Once he had established that, he could describe the mechanics of a market absent of ideology and feelings.

< >

Like many economists, Smith has been misread and misused.

In discussions about economics in the media and politics, it is often claimed that Smith said the best economic results would be achieved if everyone acted according to their own self-interest. But in reality, Smith was acutely aware that people need help from one another, and that a world where everyone chiefly thinks of themselves would be horrible to inhabit. Yet, that is not the analysis from him which has taken centre stage. Rather, he has become famous for the metaphor of 'the invisible hand', which comes from *The Wealth of Nations*. In this understanding of Smith, the hand – almost like the hand of God – will increase the wealth of a society if everyone just thinks about themselves. The hand is used to argue that self-interest is not only natural, but beneficial, and thus beyond criticism; thinking too much about the well-being of others might even be detrimental to the economy!

In fact, Smith used the concept of 'the invisible hand' only three times in his entire authorship. The historian Emma Rothschild has shown that two of these uses were clearly meant as a joke about the way that rich men exploited their poorest employees. In the third instance, Smith is saying that many businessmen would prefer to buy local rather than imported goods 'for his own security', and that they therefore would, as an 'invisible hand', advance the interests of their home nation, although that would not have been their intention. In this case, Smith is actually saying that we do *not* think only about what is cheapest, but often make social considerations when we, for example, 'buy local' to support shops in our own neighbourhoods.[6]

This is literally the opposite of how 'the invisible hand' is used today. As Joan Robinson told us earlier, we need to be careful not to be deceived by the pull of historic economic arguments in our language and culture, particularly when many of them do not have any solid basis.

'The invisible hand' is a beautiful metaphor that feels like a mixture of natural law and magic, but this phrase has been taken out of context and has taken on a life of its own. People have been clinging to this hand and still do, because it creates a sense of cosmic order in the market, a sense of optimal outcomes. Many economists continue to live and breathe for that 300-year-old hand. And we can see this in the economic debate today.

This praise of self-interest stands in striking contrast to how Smith viewed women's motivations. In *The Theory of Moral Sentiments*, Smith's first book, which deals with morality and ethics, he describes what we today might call 'the feminine touch'. He calls it humanity. He writes: 'Humanity is the virtue of a woman ... humanity consists merely in the exquisite fellow-feeling which the spectator entertains with the sentiments of the persons principally concerned, so as to grieve for their sufferings, to resent their injuries, and to rejoice at their good fortune.'[7] There is an assumption here that the care women provide is an unlimited resource, streaming from us as an unstoppable force. We can hear echoes of Locke's divine, domestic sphere. Women do not consciously calculate their sympathy for human suffering, small children, animals and the sick; their feelings are not the result of rational decision-making. Half of the world's population, then, according to Smith, is motivated by a power that is diametrically opposed to self-interest. The conclusion here is that when women provide care, it has nothing to do with competence – and therefore, it is not work. Moreover, care will never be lacking, so economists did not need to think that much about it. Care is portrayed as an unlimited resource. If a child is wailing, or a sick person needs a helping hand, or a 50-year-old moral philosopher needs his lunch, surely a woman will figure it out.

As I mentioned earlier, Smith lived with his mother, Margaret Douglas, until she died at the age of 90. For the following 12 years, Smith's cousin, Janet Douglas, looked after him. He died shortly after she did. And even though we should be wary of biographical fallacy, I think that we can glean something from Smith's descriptions of the role these women played in his life. When his mother died, he wrote in a letter to a friend: 'the final separation from a person who certainly loved me more than any other person ever did or ever will love me; and whom I certainly loved and respected more than I ever shall love or respect any other person, I cannot help feeling, even at this hour, as a very heavy stroke upon me.'[8] So, he knew. On some level, he understood perfectly well that feelings and dependence existed, that they played an essential role in people's lives, and that these feelings sprung from families, friendships and other close relationships.[9]

Smith believed that all people had goodness in them, regardless of their gender. He begins *The Theory of Moral Sentiments* with a beautiful claim. He writes: 'How selfish soever man may be supposed, there are evidently some principles in his nature which interest him in the fortune of others, and render their happiness necessary to him, though he derives nothing from it except the pleasure of seeing it.'[10] So if people prioritise themselves, they will automatically prioritise other people. For him, self-interest cannot harm others because we desire 'not only to be loved, but to be lovely'.

But this sentiment is nowhere to be found in *The Wealth of Nations*. It is hidden away in his book about morals and his private letters. And it was in the division of economics and the market on the one side and morals and the family on the other that Smith made his mark. He defined (without wanting it, I suspect) the entire field of established economics.

A SPLIT REALITY

Even though Smith's early writings are lovely, we see a tendency here that will reappear in the economic debate time and time again. What the original thinker writes is not always the same as what their thinking will be used for. Knowledge about society is a power struggle, and if you can invoke an iconic enough economist to back up your point of view, you seem more legitimate.

For Smith, the figure of the *Homo economicus* in *The Wealth of Nations* only described part of being human. But its afterlife has been very different to anything Smith could have imagined.

Think tanks are one of the main sources of economic analyses today. Unions and business interests fund the development of economic analyses that back up their positions in the public debate. One of these is the Adam Smith Institute, a British think tank. This think tank argues that the market, because of the 'invisible hand', ought to encompass all aspects of society (including care, art and more). In line with Locke, they believe that the primary task of the state is to protect free economic exchange, so the individual can do as they please. On the Adam Smith Institute's website, the split between morals and economics is in full bloom. They write: 'Smith's books are complementary: they show how self-interested human beings can live together peacefully (in the moral sphere) and productively (in the economic) ... Self-interest may drive the economy, but that is a force for good'.[11] They use Smith to support the claim that self-interest moves the economy forward, whatever the moral consequences. They then imagine a realm outside economics: 'the moral sphere'. As if economic exchange is not a part of life, as if our decisions in the market are not a reflection of who we are, but are somehow separate.

It is quite the ideological leap from Smith, who believed that humans are not only interested in themselves but also their communities, to the Adam Smith Institute, which uses Smith as a lever to argue that everyone *must* act out of self-interest in the market in order to drive the economy forward. This might seem like splitting hairs, but in this divide we find an essential struggle over who we are as humans and what kind of society is possible.

The Adam Smith Institute believes that self-interested people will create the most economically efficient society. Unethical behaviour in the market is no longer criticised but seen as a necessity. Smith is used to argue that it is 'rational' and best for everyone in the long run to put themselves first. The philosopher Seyla Benhabib describes the development well: 'An entire domain of human activity, namely, nurture, reproduction, love and care, which becomes the woman's lot in the course of the development of modern, bourgeois society, is excluded from moral and political considerations.'[12]

In her book, *Adam Smith's America*, the political economist Glory M. Liu has shown that Smith's thinking is often used as an argument for the ability of the free market to lift all boats. She recounts that in the 1950s, American editions of *The Wealth of Nations* were published without the parts where he argued for the regulation of banks and industries. Self-interest and 'the invisible hand' came to symbolise 'an entire way of thinking about society as being organized through the natural, automatic, and self-generating actions of individual economic actors'.[13] What appears as sober, neutral contributions to the economic debate can actually be propaganda, invading our culture, conversations, politics and sense of who we are.

RATIONAL INSANITY

So why did Smith paint such a reductive portrait of people and their drives in *The Wealth of Nations*, after he had praised the warmth of humanity in *The Theory of Moral Sentiments*? Because, I think, this simplification enabled a mechanical theory of the market that was easier and less complicated. Moral considerations, human connection, love, care, children, life and death got in the way of stable systems. So Smith took all the messy parts of life out of political economy and relegated them to moral philosophy, taking the ethics out of economics. He thought it was possible to create a neutral economic theory without being interpreted as if he were defending its morality. But the Adam Smith Institute is evidence of the opposite. As the anthropologist David Graeber writes in *The Utopia of Rules*: 'the moment one divides the world into two spheres in this way – into the domain of sheer technical competence and a separate domain of ultimate values – each sphere will inevitably begin trying to invade the other. Some will declare that rationality, or even efficiency, are themselves values, that they are even ultimate values, and that we should somehow create a "rational" society (whatever that means).'[14]

Smith's legacy is a view of human nature that sees the self-interested, rational man as *the* optimal foundation on which to build mechanical, economic models of society. Not optimal because this human was sympathetic or good or even realistic, but because he was good for doing mathematics, and because he appeared apolitical. Self-interest was rational because 'the invisible hand' mechanically improved the economy for everyone.

Cut to 2006, when one of the world's most famous economists, Paul Krugman, described economics' historic love of maths: 'it wasn't about ideology; it was about following the line of least mathematical resistance. Economics has always been a discipline with scientific aspirations; economists have always sought the rigor and clarity that comes from using numbers and equations to represent their ideas.'[15] But saying that something isn't ideological doesn't make it so. Taking the road of least mathematical resistance is, as we shall see, a deeply political act.

< >

When images of Spears' paparazzo attack spread across the world, only a few people mentioned that she was not alone that night. The photos depict a lonely woman with wild eyes, punching air. But if you zoom out, there are people all around: the paparazzi circled around her, desperately trying to capture her suffering so that they could profit from the pictures. This was the same paparazzi that had followed her everywhere from her debut in 1998, who in 2006 shamelessly photographed her genitalia under her dress and sold the pictures to tabloids that plastered them over their front pages.

If you zoom out even further, you'll see the record label CEOs and managers who, from Spears' first television appearance at the age of 11, seized her time, her body, her sexuality and her entire identity to wring every last dollar out of her that they could without any concern for her well-being. You see thousands of bloggers and journalists living off humiliating and degrading her for the sake of selling it as entertainment. You see the readers taking perverse pleasure in seeing a person brought to the limits of their sanity.

But back in 2007, no one was talking about how whether *these* people were crazy. Their behaviour, our behaviour, was rational, regardless of the consequences. As long as there was an economic gain, any action could be justified. We don't even notice financially driven, self-interested, ice-cold indifference to another person's suffering when it is right in our faces. We have learned that people like Spears do harm to society, and that record label CEOs bring society forward. Because they create value by selling their wares.

FEELINGS AND FACTORIES

Hobbes, Locke and Smith all fail to acknowledge that humans are fallible, fickle, mean, dumb, clever and caring. And that we are deeply interconnected, for better or worse. Throughout our lives, and especially in childhood, old age and sickness (which for many of us lasts from life's beginning to end), we are concretely dependent on other people for our survival. But among the greatest thinkers of Western intellectual history, interdependence was diametrically opposed to freedom. Because self-interest was posited as natural, those who do not act according to their own economic interests even today are portrayed as strange, while the ones who aspire to economic gains – no matter the pain they inflict – are perceived as normal.

The exclusion of domestic labour is even more significant. In order to get the mechanical gears going, these thinkers ignored the material and economic consequences of our interdependence on each other and the difficult negotiations and emotions that go along with needing one another. But two people can create something together that neither of them would be able to alone. And this happens every single day as an essential, unavoidable part of life – maybe even as life *itself*. There are not two separate spheres, a human and an economic one. There is just life.

When Adam Smith wrote that 'Nobody but a beggar chooses to depend chiefly upon the benevolence of his fellow-citizens,' he built the foundations of the dominant narrative in established economics that people who need care to survive or be happy are worthless burdens. And this also meant that the time that other people spent showing goodwill and providing care was seen as worthless. As a waste of time. Time that could have been spent advancing one's own self-interest.[16]

Spears was 'crazy' because she asked for help. That was her great sin. She made public her vulnerability, her body, and her fundamental need for respect and love. There were adults around her, and she asked them to understand her. She asked them not to exploit her. She reminded us of our mortality and about how close many of us have felt to the edge. It was as if we attacked her in order to protect ourselves. The more we distanced ourselves from her, the more rational we would appear. The Swedish feminist Samira Ariadad articulates this awful power that established economics has planted in us: 'The more we sketch the story of the human as selfish, as altruism meaning self-sacrifice, the more the empathetic subject is viewed as flawed and ill, and hence violently corrected into a normal state of apathy or egoism.'[17]

You are crazy if you ask for help, but not if you refuse to give it.

The Enlightenment thinkers did not describe the world – they shaped it. They dictated what could be expected from other people. They helped create a world view in which managers, tabloids and record company CEOs are the rational ones. In which their behaviour is 'natural', and above any criticism. In which their behaviour makes us richer, and Britney Spears' makes us poorer. They receive praise, she is humiliated.

WHAT ARE WE WORTH?

'I see it ... I got it.'

ARIANA GRANDE, '7 RINGS'

CHAPTER 4

It takes a fair amount of professional confidence to call half of the population a deficit. But it also requires trust from the reader to believe it.

This trust is a roaring success for the generation of economists that followed Smith and Locke. At the end of 1800s a group of economists, working across Europe, sought mathematical proof for a bold claim made by the British philosopher and economist Edmund Burke: 'the laws of commerce ... are the laws of nature, and consequently the laws of God.'[1] These thinkers sat at their desks, crunching numbers based on their own ideas of human psychology, decisions and desire. Every economic policy prognosis made today is underpinned by thinking from this time period. The methods are cumbersome, and for that reason, they also pose a democratic problem. Because of them, we have been duped into believing that valuation is an exact and apolitical science that can't be contested.

These ideas eventually became the microeconomic foundations of the major macroeconomic models that shape every second of your daily life.

To enter the hallowed halls of the natural sciences, economics had to become a beautiful, precise science free of feelings. Economists such as Léon Walras, William Stanley Jevons and Carl Menger – who would come to be known as the neoclassicists – took mechanics to new heights. As Jevons wrote: 'Life itself seems to be nothing but a special form of energy which is manifested in heat and electricity and mechanical force ... Must not the same inexorable reign of law which is apparent in the motions of brute matter be extended to subtle feelings of the human heart?'[2] Consequently, they turned to the science and tools of physics.

Their great breakthrough was their theory of economic equilibrium. This theory held that an economy can be in a state of perfect balance, where there are no disturbances from outside forces, and people's acts can be perfectly predicted. This, they claimed, was the natural and desirable state for the economy to be in. This theory reportedly offered mathematical proof that an economic state could exist in which the invisible hand of the market was real, giving everyone the pay that reflected their efforts and improving everyone's lives at the same time. In the spirit of Samantha

Jones in *Sex and the City*: if it sounds too good to be true, it probably is.

Many of the moral and social debates about justice and inequality that had preoccupied classical economists such as Adam Smith were discarded in favour of pure mathematics based on the self-interested *Homo economicus*. In many places, the discipline went from being called 'political economics' to simply economics. This was to be the only truly empirical social science.

The neoclassicists were behind what came to be called the marginal revolution. While physicists and chemists had stable measurements such as kilograms, grams, centimetres and volume that they could use to compare things, economists had no unit that was identical across geography, history and culture. To solve that problem, Walras, Jevons and Menger created a theory of value based on a mimicry of the natural laws of the natural sciences.[3]

But these men had a major issue when it came to finding a neutral economic measuring stick like kilograms or centimetres: value is usually related to feelings. No matter what I feel, a centimetre is a centimetre. But when it comes to products and services, one man's trash is another's treasure. They therefore determined that it is impossible to say with scientific certainty that one thing is more valuable than another.

How, then, do you ascertain whether something is bad or good for society?

Their solution was to cast the market as a 'natural' process. Supply and demand was akin to the law of gravity because people always wanted to maximise their own utility by looking out for their own self-interest. Due to this mechanical *Homo economicus*, the market supplied these economists with a scientific measure of value: prices. By this logic, you could put every person's subjective feelings about value into a market system, and the resulting prices would tell you something objective about the value of each individual object and service.

For the marginalists, prices were essential: at last, here was something like a centimetre! Now the value of a car and an apple could be compared, even though they are two completely different things. Alfred Marshall, a famous economist from this time, wrote that it was 'this definite and exact money measurement' that 'enabled economics to far outrun every other branch of the study of man'.[4]

But marginalism didn't rid us of demeaning and faulty perceptions of care and economic hierarchies. It only reinforced them and gave them a false scientific aura.[5]

THE MAGIC OF PRICES

In marginalism, people behave rationally, and markets are mechanical. We buy whatever gives us maximal utility, which is different for all of us. And because the total amount of products and services is limited, prices will reflect how many people desire or need a product, and thereby its value. More commonly, we say that 'prices are set by the law of supply and demand'.

Adam Smith posed a crucial question about supply and demand: why do diamonds cost more than water when water is so much more important? The marginalists believed they had solved this problem: because there is so much water and so few diamonds, an extra diamond has much more utility than an extra glass of water. We are willing to pay more for a diamond because there are fewer diamonds in the world than glasses of water.

If something has a high price, it is because more people want it than can get it. And therefore it must be valuable, or so the theory goes. The economist Mariana Mazzucato puts it this way: 'In their view, the supply and demand of scarce resources regulates value expressed in money. Because things exchanged in a monetary market economy have prices, price is ultimately the measure of value.'[6] It logically follows from this theory, of course, that if something doesn't have a price, it doesn't have value – and the theory of marginalism meant that this could now be claimed as an objective fact. An entire sphere outside the market was suddenly deemed worthless.[7]

Marginalism built on the Enlightenment tradition of seeing people as 'free' and, as Hobbes believed, mathematical individuals without bodies with basic needs. In this system, there is no way to address the fundamental difference between water and diamonds – that you will die without water, but not without diamonds. Even though you might have a physical disability, in the eyes of marginalism, a wheelchair is a product like any other. The same rules apply to all products, no matter the role they play in the life of the consumer.

This missing distinction between desires and basic needs was to some extent intentional. These economists didn't want to stray too far into a philosophical discussion about human rights because that would be political. They didn't want to get mixed up in what it actually takes for different kinds of people to enter the market and trade. So they left the matter of what keeps us healthy, happy and alive to supply and demand. This tracks with the idea of negative rights that we explored in the previous chapter. You have the right to use the money you've earned to purchase what will be most useful to you. And the amount of money you've earned is fair because it is determined by supply and demand. It all works, supposedly.

Many economists have since criticised the way that marginalism reduces everything to utility. The economist Frank Knight was already putting up a fight in 1921 when he wrote that we live 'in a world where individuals are born naked, destitute, helpless, untrained and must spend a third of their lives in acquiring the prerequisites of a free contractual existence.'[8]

When you use an enlightened, rational, omnipotent individual as the basis for your theory, there will be many situations you won't be able to account for. Some instances of this are obvious: when we're children, mentally struggling, living with addiction, lack full information or are so ill that we do not have time to act perfectly rationally. Another example is when we simply act stupidly, get tricked by commercials or fail to understand what would be best for us. I imagine many of you, like me, find these scenarios familiar.[9]

It probably won't come as a surprise that the theories developed by Walras, Menger, Jevons and others around this time were conceived behind a desk; a market in equilibrium, inhabited by rational actors, simply doesn't exist in reality. It never has, and never will. It is paradoxical indeed that at the very time economists wanted to mimic the natural sciences, they retreated from empirical reality and into pure theory. Freudian jokesters have called it physics envy.

And we could ask ourselves: where exactly did those diamonds come from that were used in Smith's example? It was, for the most part, men from African countries, toiling in harrowing conditions for almost no pay. But when value is based on the price at the time of purchase, production falls out of view. You can suddenly talk about the value of a diamond without talking about who found it, or what it cost their bodies, communities and their natural environment. Numbers become more real than reality.

In *Visions of Inequality*, the economist Branko Milanović writes that after the adoption of the notion of equilibrium, 'Whether endowments were acquired through previous market transactions, pillage, exploitation, inheritance, monopoly or whatever other means was not the subject of economics as the science of relative prices … economics became the science of the present … the social relations underpinning capitalism were entirely ignored.'[10]

The theory of equilibrium and the rational actor has received plenty of critique, and the academic field of microeconomics has since moved in new directions.

But the legacy of the beautiful and fair invisible hand remains embedded in established macroeconomics and in our culture.

SMOOTH OPERATORS

The economists who were convinced by the marginal revolution's take on society had, and still have, an extremely difficult time describing goods and services that did not have a market price, and they often just fell out of view. The market became the most elegant way both to distribute resources and to figure out what things were worth. The market, in other words, worked *for* the economists and sent them signals. One of the signals they are currently reading is that women are an economic deficit for society. This is because women tend to sell their labour at a lower price than many men. If a nurse makes £2,000 a month and a banker makes £10,000, the banker is five times as valuable.

Marginalism's decision to measure value at the time of purchase was groundbreaking for economics at the time. In the preceding decades, some believed value could be determined by the time spent producing a product, others by the natural resources consumed, and others by how the product or service ended up being used. Many economists in the nineteenth century would probably be stunned to hear how powerful marginalist theories have become.

In 1825, William Thompson and Anna Wheeler offered another perspective. They belonged to a group of thinkers who called themselves 'utopian socialists'. In the *Appeal of One Half of the Human Race* they pleaded their case that domestic labour should be evenly distributed between the sexes because it created economic value and served a central function in society. They did not believe that the market could be used to measure value. There could be value without a price, and prices where there wasn't any value to speak of.

Thompson and Wheeler were worried that men's higher income led them to overestimate their own worth. As they write: 'Superiority in the production or accumulation of individual wealth will ever be whispering into man's ear preposterous notions of his relative importance over woman.'[11] They believed that the theories in which prices and pay were indicative of value gave a higher cultural status to certain people that didn't deserve it (and a lower status to some who deserved better!).

According to Wheeler and Thompson, the distribution of resources in society had more to do with power, culture and exploitation than any beautiful, indisputable natural law. But their argument could not be described with mathematical formulas and mechanical models. Marginalism could. The pair lost the fight.

It is often conveniently forgotten that Léon Walras, probably the most famous marginalist, identified as a socialist and in fact believed that it *was* possible to intervene in the forces of the market: 'Because gravity is a natural fact and obeys natural laws, it does not follow that we can never do anything but watch its action.'[12] And he was a huge fan of state-funded public transport! But these arguments were philosophical, not mathematical.[13] Instead, what lived on from Walras was that the market was the most optimal way of distributing resources and measuring their value.

These assumptions hum beneath today's political and economic debates. It is not unusual for people to criticise taxes because taxes 'take money' from those who 'work the hardest' and 'create the most value'. These are echoes of an old and influential quote by Margaret Thatcher, the former Conservative prime minister of the United Kingdom, when she decried the practice of having taxes pay for services like public care work: 'Socialist governments traditionally do make a financial mess. They always run out of other people's money.'[14] But we could flip it around and say that a market economy with no welfare state will eventually run out of other people's free care work (or nature's free resources). All economic systems shuffle value around. But when we only glance at prices the shuffling of unpaid care becomes invisible, and the value of paid care can end up being distorted and obscured.

Hidden behind any form of paid labour and priced item lies the care work that makes it possible. And every form of paid labour has social consequences that aren't captured by its price.

In 2009, the New Economics Foundation investigated the value of work by looking at its contribution to society instead of its price. They called it 'social value'. This included the residual effects of the work, the effect on the environment, and what it made possible elsewhere in society.[15] In the world of banking, £7 of social value was lost for every pound earned. Nannies, who received a far lower salary, created up to £9.50 in value for each pound they earned, namely because they made it possible for parents to work and helped raise new labourers. Sanitation workers, including refuse collectors, created up to £12 in social value. Are pay and prices really reflective of value? To put it mildly, nobody knows.

TOO MUCH OF A GOOD THING

In 1954, the economists Kenneth Arrow and Gérard Debreu created a mathematical model to describe general equilibrium in the market and gave marginalism a makeover.[16] They claimed that equilibrium would ensure that supply and demand set prices that would let everyone buy exactly what they needed, and that unemployment would always be a choice (*If it sounds too good to be true, it probably is ...*). For Arrow and Debreu, the market is where people meet their needs. We are kept healthy, happy and alive by the things and services we buy.

This claim has had an outsized influence on economic thinking, and many economics textbooks start with a definition that goes something like this: 'Economics is the study of how people allocate their limited resources to satisfy their unlimited wants.'

Simply put, people are never satisfied, but the closer we get to equilibrium, the closer we get to satisfaction. Arrow and Debreu wrote that a market in equilibrium would, in theory, increase *social welfare*. The theory didn't have much to say about the needs that were met outside the market. And there was nothing about where people came from. Yet another mushroom plot!

In Arrow and Debreu's theory, companies exist because they increase consumer utility (welfare). But in my Instagram feed, for example, I don't see companies that are answering real demands or making people particularly happy. I see companies that spend millions on ads, influencing and using subtle manipulation to *create* a demand. I wouldn't want any of these products if I had no idea that they existed.

If only the marginalists had gone to a bar, where some holier-than-thou teenager inspired by *Fight Club* had scribbled on the bathroom wall: 'We work jobs we hate so we can buy shit we don't need to impress people we don't even like.' Marginalists actually thought that we derive happiness from the things we buy. But what's available on the market is often an expression of a desire for something else. There is something hidden behind the product – something you could probably find elsewhere, if circumstances were different.

One study from 2017, which looked at Denmark and Canada, among other places, showed that the things we spend money on that make us happiest are those that give us more time, like a dishwasher or a vacuum cleaner.[17] Another study of some of the wealthiest shoppers in the world found that 77 per cent of those who buy luxury goods buy expensive products purely to be part of a community.[18] People will spend thousands to see Taylor Swift, Beyoncé or Kendrick Lamar live. We gladly spend money to take part in something gigantic, shared, beautiful. This has a lot of value. But in contrast to the marginalist perspective, these 'products' aren't necessarily things we take from one another, but rather things that we share with one another, at the same time as getting something from the experience, too. Valuable products aren't always diamonds; they can be greater and better because they are shared. Something can have utility precisely because you can share it with other people.

On the surface, house-cleaning items, luxury goods and concerts look like simple desires satisfied in the marketplace. But behind each lies other needs: more time to spend with friends and family, recognition from a community of like-minded people, or belting out a song you love with a crowd. You can also find these things for free. But in marginalism, one doesn't talk about social or shared value. It is only the utility of the good that matters, and that utility is linked to the individual.

RIGID FUTURES

In established economics and especially in the media, it is an accepted truth that it is possible to 'predict' the societal consequences of various economic policies.

However, the assumptions of human behaviour required to make those predictions are rarely acknowledged. Across the globe, whenever a decision is made, economists, politicians and journalists ask whether a policy is 'optimal'. But is there ever an apolitical or neutral answer to what is optimal?

This dream of predicting the future was a long held one, especially by Léon Walras and William Stanley Jevons. While powerful economists both before and after the marginalists knew that neither people nor economists behave according to the rules, the beauty of the equation was tempting. Marginalism helped economics get the central role in political decision-making that it holds today.

When you hear about the assumptions that underpin many economic models of reality, it makes sense that established economics has kept them under wraps. I think many people would be pretty surprised if they knew the truth.

In the introduction to their economic textbook from 1995, the economists Paul Samuelson and William Nordhaus discuss what it actually takes to make those predictive graphs about the future that are served up to us every day. They write: 'What we assume in consumer demand theory is that consumers are reasonably consistent in their tastes and actions.

We expect that people do not flail around and make themselves miserable by constantly making mistakes. If most people act consistently most of the time, avoiding erratic changes in buying behaviour and generally choosing their most preferred bundles, our theory of demand will provide a reasonably good approximation to the facts.'[19] These shaky grounds eventually became the microeconomic foundation of macroeconomics. These are the assumptions we never see. That everyone has to behave like clairvoyant robots.

What Samuelson and Nordhaus tell us here is essential to established economics. Economic models have to simplify reality to an extreme degree to be able to make claims about the economy as a whole. This is no precise, empirical science. Many economic calculations in politics assume that people never make bad choices, that they will want the same thing in ten years as they do today, and that they are entirely unaffected by advertising or trends.

Do you know *anyone* who doesn't make themselves miserable by constantly making mistakes? It's all I do! As the economist Robert Skidelsky writes: 'Humans are an endless disappointment to economists. They mess up their equations.'[20]

One of the founders of marginalism, William Stanley Jevons, who spent many years in Australia in the

1850s, wrote about the Indigenous populations in his masterwork, *The Theory of Political Economy*. He said that 'savages' have a poor sense of time management, refuse to work and are unable to make long-term decisions about their money. In other words, they liked relaxing and weren't particularly interested in following the dictates of a clock. So, to make his marginalist theory about human nature function, Jevons created a 'fictive average' based on the image of what he perceived as the civilised Englishman. In his later book, *The Principles of Science* (1874), he goes on to say that this person should be taken as a 'hypothetical simplification of a problem'.[21] This simplification of a problem (the problem is real people) is something we'll encounter again in the major, modern economic models. Jevons' treatment of the Indigenous populations is instructive because it shows how theory can be prescriptive, when it purports to be descriptive. If these so-called 'savages' wanted to avoid the very concrete violence and injustice that colonialism entailed, they had to demonstrate a behaviour that fit the dominant economic theories: self-interest, mechanical, disciplined work and trade on the market.

To stop human beings from being such a disappointment, the theories of general equilibrium have sometimes been used to shape society. Those who make the theories see themselves as superior to culture, while in truth they create the culture and disguise it as an expression of human nature.[22]

A 'PURE' VIEW OF AN IMPURE WORLD

Marginalism intensified the problems of the Enlightenment. We lost the ability to describe the indirect creation of value between individuals and things without a price.

Nancy Folbre has spent her career in economics tracing the role of women. She argues that from around 1900, it was seen as a scientific fact in established economics that women got something out of being married to a man, because he earned money, but that neither men nor society got anything from the work women performed at home. The home had gone from being mushrooms and God to being a burden of unpriced activities.[23]

The problem that established economics has with care work is not that it is primarily performed by women. It is that economists' view of themselves as 'scientists' sometimes results in a distaste for the unpredictable, unpriced things that come from culture, care and human relationships, not only in the home, but throughout society.[24]

Many economists do not believe that their work has anything to do with what is 'good' or 'bad', but only to objective facts about how to optimise the market and thereby increase social welfare. In 1996, the economist Julie Nelson suggested that the consequences of this for established economics was that 'The study of markets and the use of mathematical models of individual self-interest, for example, are at the core of the academic discipline, while the study of families and the use of verbal models of social structure and other interests are considered as, at best, barely within the realm of economics.'[25]

Due to this, many economic models struggle to take into account the ways in which our lives can be shaped by circumstances outside our control. Structural inequities between people can suddenly appear as results of free choices made by rational actors. There are extreme examples of this, such as when the British member of Parliament Suella Braverman said that being homeless was a lifestyle choice.[26] But it can also crop up in much more subtle ways. The economist Lourdes Benería has observed that established economics has struggled with gender inequality as a result of culture and violent oppression.[27] Instead, inequality has at times appeared to be the result of pure, free choice. If men weren't looking after children and cooking dinner, and women weren't well represented on the labour market, then that must reflect their own desires or lack of skills, not discrimination, violence, or structural barriers.

There is one study I'm reminded of whenever the conversation turns to marginalism, rationality and value. In 2021, two economists, Maddalena Ronchi and Nina Smith, found that Danish women receive higher salaries in the private sector after their male bosses have had their first daughter.[28] Male bosses suddenly find that the work done by their female employees is more valuable once they have their own little girl running around at home. This poses a problem for marginalist theory: the amount we are willing to pay for something on the market (in this case, female labour) can be determined by something entirely external to performance. It also means that demand isn't always determined by how much utility we gain from something. Labour prices, for example, can easily be affected by individuals' culturally distorted perceptions of how skilled an employee is. Apparently, once you have a daughter, it's easier to see the value in the contributions of other women.

Typically, problems like the pay discrimination based on gender described above are called 'market failures' in established economics. How ingenious that a discipline can call something they repeatedly observe 'a failure'. How can reality be a failure? And how many times can a theory fail before it is discarded and replaced with another?

Gender discrimination is just one of the many 'market failures' that marginalism has encountered. In fact, the claim that prices reflect the value that customers assign to their purchases is highly contested. In 2023, economists Isabella Weber and Evan Wasner proved that, when inflation skyrocketed in the US during 2021, many companies had raised their prices – not because of increased costs, better products or higher demand, but simply because they could get away with it. Consumers accepted the higher prices because they thought inflation was the cause. Windfall profits for the companies followed.[29,30] As the political theorist Jonathan Schlefer writes in *The Assumptions Economists Make*, there is no proof that a market in equilibrium increases social welfare, fairly allocates goods or accurately sets prices according to their value.[31] Equilibrium has never existed. It is a fantasy that billions of people's robot behaviour will act as an invisible hand, pushing things towards equilibrium. The economist Frank Ackerman has written that: 'The mathematical failure of general equilibrium is such a shock to established theory that it is hard for many economists to absorb its full impact.'[32] This certainly seems to be the case, as the most used macroeconomic models in the world are still based on the assumption that equilibrium can be used to say something worthwhile about reality. Almost every calculation of the consequences of economic policy that shapes your everyday life rests on assumptions about the economy that do not hold up to closer scrutiny.[33]

Faith in the theory of equilibrium has been catastrophic for care. Neither unpaid nor paid care work are assumed to play a role in the creation of labour or products. The market stands alone as the place we go to meet our needs. The prices set become the most important factor in understanding something or someone's role in the economy, and the maintenance of human life disappears from sight.[34]

PRICES AND REALITY

The idea that established economics can neutrally determine value and predict the future without shaping it is one of the primary reasons that economics has become as powerful as it has, despite the fact that it is constantly confronted with evidence to the contrary.

In 2007, the Danish economist Jakob Brøchner Madsen was interviewed for *Berlingske Tidende*. He believed that a financial crisis was imminent; banks had given people larger and larger loans that they could no longer repay. The interview was titled: 'Now what, professor?'[35] It was meant to be mocking, as in, haha, where's the financial crisis? Wasn't it right around the corner? Brøchner Madsen responded that it would come soon enough. The interview portrayed him as stupid because no other economists agreed with him. In the end he said: 'Sometimes you have to remember that most of the chief economists you'll encounter are extremely eloquent, but they have never seen a shred of science.' Six months later, the global economy collapsed because of precisely the kind of loans Brøchner Madsen had raised the alarm about.

In November 2008 Queen Elizabeth II asked a group of economists at the London School of Economics why none of them saw the financial crisis coming.[36] They responded in a letter, explaining that the smartest economists often look at distinct aspects of the economy rather than 'the bigger picture'. Very reassuring.

The Danish Economic Council's growth projections have turned out to be true on average one out of every 35 times. In the past 40 years, their prognoses have not become more accurate.[37]

In 2023 the Danish economist Anne Sophie Lassen was asked by *Dagbladet Information* to put a price on unpaid domestic labour.[38] She explained that economics has two available methods she could choose from.

One was based on input, the other on output. With the input-based method, time spent on these tasks could be priced according to the parent's normal job, an average Danish hourly rate, or could be based on what a daycare teacher or similar professional would make doing the same work. The output-based method would look at what this unpaid work 'produced': a kilo of clean clothes, or a dinner. These were the only two options. True to the marginalist spirit, both compared activities in the home to market prices, which were supposed to offer a form of truth. Neither the input nor output methods tell us anything about the human value this work creates for those performing and receiving it, or about the value it creates for society in the long term in the form of the creation of new workers.

Lassen concluded: 'Economics has a very limited vocabulary to describe the long-term effects of care and close relationships, but maybe this too much to ask?' Clearly, it is a big ask. But it seems a fair one of the discipline shaping every aspect our future.

WORTHLESS MAINTENANCE

'I need not sell my soul to buy bliss. I have an inward treasure, born with me, which can keep me alive if all extraneous delights should be withheld; or offered only at a price I cannot afford to give.'
CHARLOTTE BRONTË, JANE EYRE

CHAPTER 5

The most common question asked of feminist economists is whether we are advocating for pricing everything that is currently priceless. If prices are the only language accepted in policy, should we attempt to price the value of sharing a joke with friends? Should a kiss from your wife cost £3? Should you send your grandchild an invoice after Christmas? I'd rather not be the bearer of more bad news, but prices are already being assigned to everything in politics. It's just mostly happening behind closed doors.

Just because friendship, love, nature, free time, volunteer work, a smile, sleep and relaxation don't have exact prices doesn't mean that we have collectively decided that these things are invaluable and inviolable. It doesn't mean that we have unanimously declared that life's inexpressible pleasures can't be measured, or that every political calculation should allocate an infinity symbol to everything without a price.

In reality, these priceless joys have been assigned an implicit number: zero. In the language that shapes our politics, these things are often worthless. The solution isn't to put a price on them, but rather to acknowledge that value is not a scientific question but a political one that can only be answered democratically.

In 2023, many Danes discovered just how easy it is to get rid of priceless things when the established economy is allowed to determine value. The Danish government decided to revoke a national holiday called Great Prayer Day. A long weekend in the spring was suddenly a regular, short one. The economic gains of an extra workday were furiously debated. The Minister for Finance claimed it would give the state an extra 3.2 billion kroner.[1] Meanwhile, the chief economic adviser in the Economic Council, Carl-Johan Dalgaard, argued that this number had been pulled out of thin air: 'I have not seen any evidence that getting rid of a holiday will result in any significant improvement in the national economy.'[2]

People speculated widely about the gains of an extra day of work, but not about what would be given up. That was impossible. I thought about what I had lost. The fun Thursday night, when you know you can sleep in the next day; a slightly longer lunch maybe; a walk if the weather was nice. How much more had we lost as a society? What relationships, conversations and meetings would not happen now? In established economics, people disagree about things as measurable as the value of extra work hours. But there is no scientifically accepted language for the lunch, the walk, the beer in the sun. How are we supposed to fight for something when its value can't be measured?

A RISING INFLUENCE

In the years preceding and following the Second World War, the universities were abuzz, developing models to describe everything from consumers to corporate behaviour. Few of these theories were inspired by marginalism. In fact, multiple influential thinkers at this time thought marginalism was a total dead-end.

During this period, the economist John Maynard Keynes became very powerful. Keynes was sceptical of the infallibilities of the market. He called economics a moral science and believed that we *could* in fact say that some things are 'good' and valuable to people, independent of their prices.[3] These were what he called non-economic things: love, beauty and truth.[4] Economists and sociologists like Seebohm Rowntree and William Beveridge and most of their contemporaries rejected marginalism. During the brief period lasting from around the 1930s to the 1970s, these thinkers created entirely different established perceptions of the national economy to the one that is dominant today. They believed that the market should be regulated to create more equality between people and prevent unemployment, and that access to education and healthcare was necessary to create a good, sustainable society. It was an accepted truth in economics at this time that state investments could catalyse growth in the private sector. It was also during this period that the welfare state spread across Europe and to a certain extent the United States. Neoclassical economics fell out of fashion. But don't worry: *they'll be back.*

With the start of the Second World War, there was a serious need to figure out how to do things as cheaply as possible, and economists were given essential problems to solve, particularly those hailing from the Allied Powers.[5] Models and calculations became so important that the economist Paul Samuelson called the Second World War 'the economists' war'.[6] During the war, economists taught politicians a new tool (as we'll see, a main character in this book!): cost-benefit analysis. This is a way to calculate how to do something as cheaply as possible, with the greatest yield. Economics was well-suited to this kind of war equation because every body is the same when you're trying to kill it, and everything takes place in the short term. It is only when people need to be kept healthy, happy and alive in the long term that cost-benefit analysis begins to fall short.[7]

These economic methods were a smash hit and became central after the Allies won. The Allies wanted to build a new world order with the aim of preventing a new war – and of solidifying their power. Political leaders of the winning nations decided that international trade was one of the most important keys to lasting peace. To put this system in motion, however, it was necessary to be able to compare national economies, and therefore everyone had to speak the same economic language. In the newly created United Nations, gross domestic product (GDP) was chosen in 1946 as the new metric that would make this possible. GDP was developed by the economist Simon Kuznets and was based on thinking from Keynes and the economist Arthur Cecil Pigou. It was introduced as a requirement for all member nations of the UN. GDP is one of the most significant consequences of the marginal revolution and its focus on prices. But as we now know, prices can be deceptive.

ONE NUMBER TO RULE THEM ALL

GDP is a combined measure of the prices of all the goods and services that have been purchased over a period of time, typically a year, by individuals, companies and the state (there are many minor variations, but this is the most standard definition). This is then called the size of the economy. GDP is usually divided by the total population into GDP per capita and the higher the resulting number is, the more developed the society, or so we are told. Initially, GDP did not include anything without a price, but if something doesn't have a price today, the input or output method mentioned in the previous chapter can be used to approximate a price based on market comparisons. This is the case, for example, with homegrown food or livestock.[8] The price of a good or service is also more significant here than what the good or service *does*. In the eyes of GDP, a CEO who

GOODS, SERVICES, AND INVESTMENTS THAT ARE BOUGHT AND SOLD FOR MONEY	EVERYTHING THAT ISN'T ON THE MARKET, INCLUDING UNPAID CARE WORK, NATURAL RESOURCES AND PROCESSES

To the left is GDP. The dividing line is the 'production line'. Everything to the left is productive and everything to the right is unproductive. The old economics joke goes that if you marry your maid, she moves from left to right.

earns 100,000 kroner a month is better than a nurse who earns 26,000 kroner a month. And it's better if you spend an hour at work than an hour with your friends.

Whenever you hear a politician say that something increases or decreases growth, they are talking about GDP. In *The Value of Everything*, Mariana Mazzucato summarises: 'GDP, for instance, does not clearly distinguish a cost from an investment in future capacity, such as research and development; services valuable to the economy such as "care" may be exchanged without any payment, making them invisible to GDP calculators ... a resource that is destroyed by pollution may not be counted as a subtraction from GDP – but when pollution is cleaned up by marketed services, GDP increases.'[9]

GDP, in other words, doesn't notice if we lose something without a price. From the 1960s onwards, GDP has shaped many geopolitical hierarchies. Some have even argued that GDP is more important than military power.[10] GDP defines what counts as a 'developing country'. It also dictates who makes important decisions in powerful international organisations like the OECD, G7 and G20.[11]

GDP is not a neutral measurement. It has provoked hefty debate from day one. In the years that followed the introduction of GDP, it was already receiving criticism. Simon Kuznets himself said in 1962 that 'distinctions must be kept in mind between quantity and quality of growth, between its costs and return, and between the short and the long run ... goals for "more" growth should specify more growth of what and for what.'[12]

The adoption of GDP has had massive geopolitical consequences, particularly for formerly colonised nations in the Global South. In these countries, a lot of economic activity did not take place on the market, and many 'unused' natural resources weren't counted towards GDP because they were not sold as products. In countries such as Egypt, people were shocked to realise in the 1950s that they, because of GDP, were suddenly seen as 'underdeveloped' overnight.[13]

During the development of GDP, the economist Phyllis Deane's proposal to include more things without prices in alternate ways that could have changed the representation of formerly colonised countries was rejected.[14] Some Western economies were concerned that doing so might give these countries the impression that they had the resources and wealth to ask for more freedom. The historian Frederick Cooper writes about this power struggle in the United Nations in his book *Africa since 1940*, arguing that GDP was used in its early days as an argument against withdrawing from colonised regions.[15] Previously, colonialism had been justified by claiming that the colonised populations were culturally regressive. GDP meant that these countries could now be categorised as *economically* regressive, too. GDP made it easier to argue that these 'underdeveloped' countries needed to be developed by the 'rich' countries, who, in exchange, could use their resources and labour much as they pleased.

The consequences of GDP's rising power were felt wherever things and activities couldn't be quantified. This included domestic labour. Both Phyllis Deane and her boss, the economist Richard Stone, had to admit that it was extremely difficult to calculate the value of housework using the existing economic methods. So, they didn't. Stone wrote about its exclusion: 'This treatment is not a matter of principle but convenience … Attempts to extend the production boundary by valuing household and amateur activities come up against an almost complete lack of information.'[16] It wasn't that household or other unpaid activities didn't matter or didn't have value. It was simply that the tools being used could not do the job they were made for: understanding a country's value creation.

DEAD NUMBERS WALKING

Many economists would probably argue that these critiques of GDP are dated, and that its problems have long since sunk in. The problem is that GDP continues to play a central role from the very top of geopolitics to the local level. It holds both economic and cultural power, despite being fundamentally flawed. The economist Diane Coyle dryly noted in 2014 that, 'Although we economists have always known in theory that GDP does not measure social welfare in any sense, we – and therefore policy makers and news commentators – have always ignored that caveat in practice. For decades now we have been taking the growth of GDP as our measure of whether we are growing more prosperous or better off in a wider sense.'[17] It is an odd state of affairs, certainly.

From major to local politics, GDP is written into our legislative processes. The EU keeps a close eye on how much money a state can borrow, and this amount is dependent on that country's GDP. Therefore an increase in GDP is always good, regardless of what it means for the citizens, because then the country can borrow more. As a result, a number of European politicians sighed in relief in 2014 when the EU decided that sex work and narcotics would now be part of GDP. Suddenly their national debt looked much smaller than it had the previous day. They were now a little further from breaking EU financial law. The United Kingdom's GDP increased by 4.6 per cent – no less than £65 billion – because of narcotics and sex work.[18]

National debt based on GDP determines whether a country is seen as 'stable' on the financial markets. If its loans are too large as a percentage of GDP, and the market's trust in that country's economy begins to waver, it will become more expensive for that nation to borrow money because its interest rates will increase.[19] This is particularly true of countries with weaker currencies. Yes, that's right: the richer a country is, the cheaper it is for it to borrow money. This means that a country like Denmark pays dramatically less in interest than a country like Kenya. For this reason, the Danish Economic Council was worried during the financial crisis that Denmark's loans could create a 'risk of a negative spiral in which a major debt would lead to higher interest rates, which would cause greater debt, and so on.'[20] You need to keep GDP growing, not necessarily because of what it does inside the economy, but because of how it *looks* to people evaluating it from the outside.

EU legislation also limits the annual public spending deficit. In Denmark, this limit was set at 0.5 per cent of our GDP for many years. Our public spending could not exceed this percentage, no matter the consequences. Despite massive protests from – in particular – workers in the care sector, this number has been unshakeable, often with reference to EU fiscal rules.

But when the war in Ukraine broke out, the limit in Denmark was raised to 1 per cent.[21] When weapons needed to be purchased, it was suddenly okay to have a much larger deficit. This is not unusual in established economic thinking. According to EU financial legislation, countries can exceed deficit limits if the money will be used to build bridges or houses or to procure weapons (this is called 'capital stock').[22] But it isn't okay to exceed the deficit limit if the money will be spent on salaries for nurses, teachers or doctors. Weapons are an investment. Care is an expense.

This makes long-term, significant investments in health, education and care more difficult to achieve; they often require a large contribution up front. It is currently illegal in EU countries for politicians not to take GDP size into account when they propose policies. Every single penny spent on public childcare is influenced by the size of GDP. Many economists agree that GDP shouldn't be a primary political metric. But it is.

PEOPLE NEED MAINTENANCE

One afternoon in 1980s New York, the economist Marilyn Waring felt like she was losing her mind. She had spent a few weeks at the United Nations library reading *The System of National Accounts* (SNA), which describes how GDP is calculated. She discovered that women's unpaid care work was not included in GDP anywhere in the world. She had found out that domestic labour was categorised as 'free time' or 'inactivity' for 'practical reasons' – meaning it would be too difficult to include. In the eyes of GDP, taking care of a flock of kids and taking a nap are equivalent. Either way, you are unproductive. Waring became one of the most important critics of GDP, and in 1988 she published her book *Counting for Nothing*, which influenced millions of feminists but unfortunately had little influence on the established economy. This is one of the main reasons that women continue to be a 'deficit to society'. Across the globe they spend more time than men taking care of children without being paid to do so.

Denmark is one of the most gender equal countries in the world, but even here women spend 54 minutes more on average on unpaid domestic labour per day than men. That corresponds to roughly seven hours more per week. Globally, women perform about 76 per cent of all unpaid domestic labour, and in so-called developing countries, women do 80 per cent of this work, compared to 65 per cent in developed countries.[23]

Let's look at the consequences for Danish women, as an example. As soon as women have children, they earn less, and this impacts their tax contributions and their contributions to GDP. For the rest of their lives, women with children earn 20 per cent less than men in similar jobs. Men's working lives are essentially unchanged by having children. Those extra 54 minutes don't include all the coordinating that takes place outside the home, which is often called the *mental load*. This includes setting up playdates, planning dinner, checking the school intranet and structuring the week. Across Europe, women forego 242 billion euros in income as a result of the unequal division of household work. One Danish study showed that the amount of stress hormones in the body rises for women when they come home from work. Men's decreases.[24]

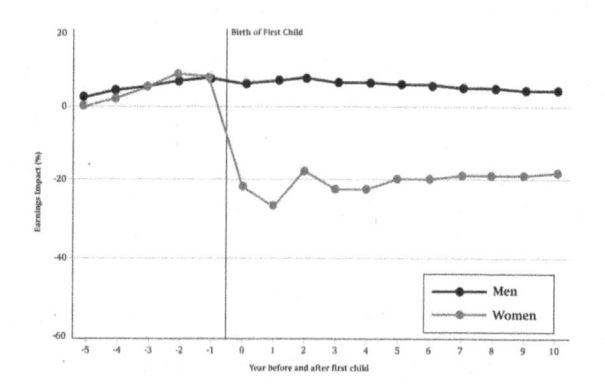

Two tragedies. From Henrik Kleven, Camille Landais and Jakob Egholt Søgaard. 'Children and Gender Inequality: Evidence from Denmark', *American Economic Journal: Applied Economics*, 2019.

This unpaid work is entirely invisible in GDP because it is not sold on the market. GDP can tell us plenty about new things that are produced and sold, but it struggles to account for everything to do with reproduction, or what we could call maintenance – taking care of existing people and things.

This is why more growth is created by purchasing formula than breastfeeding. More growth is created by buying a new shirt instead of repairing an old one. More growth is created by being at work than by singing a child a lullaby before bed. And more growth is created by chopping down a tree and selling a bench than letting the tree be. Everything without a price is subject to the same fate in this equation. As John Locke wrote: 'land that is left wholly to nature, that has no improvement of pasturage, tillage or planting, is called, as indeed it is, waste; and we shall find the benefit of it amounts to little more than nothing.'[25] This passage from Locke was essential to Jevons' understanding of the 'savage' Aboriginal people of Australia. If you didn't exploit nature for profit and self-interest, then you weren't civilised. Equating value and prices bolstered the Europeans' argument for colonising land and people. The colonised had been wasting the land, whereas Europeans were turning it into value.

Feminists working at the intersection of gender, climate and economics have argued that reproductive work in the home and natural resources share the same economic fate. This branch of thinking is called ecofeminism. GDP, namely, sees the maintenance of people and nature as worthless. Tithi Bhattacharya, associate professor of history at Purdue University, has called this an 'undermin[ing of] the very infrastructures of life-making', and describes how the language of economics has made it impossible to fight for reproductive work.[26] We never register what we lose when we take time and trees from people and the planet and sell them as products. In a cost-benefit analysis, it will always look like things that are priceless are not lost. We become richer in things, but poorer in all that can't be measured, Bhattacharya writes.

SPLIT APART

In 2013, the consulting firm Trucost was asked to estimate the global amount of 'unpriced natural capital', including things like clean water, land, clean air and all the resources that companies use without paying market price for it. The result was a report called *Natural Capital at Risk*. Trucost concluded that the sectors they analysed used a total of $4.7 trillion of the planet's resources per year for free. Not one of the top 20 most resource-intensive sectors would make a profit if they paid the market price for the resources they use and the nature they destroy.[27] These sectors *only* make a profit because nature is free.

Many economists have acknowledged that this state of affairs challenges marginalism's core claim, which is that companies create value, not destroy it. As a result, Denmark has implemented a so-called green GDP in an attempt to price natural resources.[28] This is what economist Peter Birch Sørensen was talking about when he so aptly described the power of GDP and prices in politics: 'Understandably, many people probably find it strange to put a price tag on the song of a lark. But if we don't, important environmental values risk being underprioritized in the political process.'[29]

The process behind calculating green GDP demonstrates in its simplicity just how limited the methods of established economics are when it comes to assessing value. The method goes as follows: you ask people what they would pay to protect an area, a species or a plant, and use this to ascertain the value of every individual part of nature. This is called environmental economics. We now encounter another 'market failure': the destruction of the environment and pollution are understood as being, like discrimination, another area where the market fails to price according to value, so we must make up a way to find a real price. These prices should then be implemented and hopefully bring you closer to equilibrium.[30] Pricing nature through questionnaires and interviews seems to me like putting a band-aid on an open fracture. Let's see how it works in practice.

In 2005, residents of the Danish town of Silkeborg and others across the country were asked by environmental economists about their feelings towards building a new highway around the town. They found: 'Results show that respondents in general have strong preferences, i.e. high willingness to pay, for protecting forests and wetlands against motorway encroachment whereas protection of heaths is less important.'[31] The results show that these people, of course having no knowledge of biology or biodiversity to speak of, have no choice but to price nature using vibes. In a note, the economists running the project wrote that biologists believe heaths to be the most important habitat for biodiversity. Too bad!

I think that many biologists would find it appalling to set prices on elements of the natural world based on human preferences. Nature, after all, is known for being symbiotic. Heaths and forests are not separate entities – they need one another.

In 2019, two Danish CEOs wrote an op-ed in the Danish newspaper *Berlingske* in which they said, 'Clean water, air, nature and biodiversity, along with a sustainable climate, are vital and fundamental to us all,' and that access to these resources should be enshrined in law. They continue: 'We can do this by adding green rights to the Constitution.'[32] This would make nature a positive right by law, by protecting it from exploitation by humans and companies. In a blog post about the proposal, professor of economics Christian Bjørnskov wrote that his 'immediate thought was that these two guys had eaten or smoked something funny'.[33] He was implying that positive rights such as the 'right to nature' are undemocratic because they force people to do something that they might not want to – for example, to protect heaths. Bjørnskov didn't mention that we are all currently being forced to live on a planet that is treated as if it is worthless.

The absence of care for nature is perceived as freedom, while the presence of care for nature is perceived as restrictive. The absence of care itself is neutral and apolitical. The presence of care is emotional and political.

It is not difficult to see how nature and unpaid care work become fellow sufferers under the rules of GDP. Unpriced natural resources contribute value to the 'productive' part of the economy in which goods and services have a price.³⁴ But you can't measure how much value they contribute because these resources are 'free'. So we take and take and take until these resources are exhausted, impoverished and dead. Maybe there is not such a big difference between a dead ocean and a person diagnosed with burnout: both have pumped value into economic production without having time and resources for their own reproduction. But what it has really cost them, we cannot see.

Many economists have noticed the problem of domestic labour and have attempted to put a price on it, as with nature. This method most often involves multiplying the minimum wage by the number of hours that people physically spend in their homes doing tasks that they could, in theory, hire others to do for them. In 2006, two economists in Finland calculated what the value of unpaid care work would be according to this metric. They landed on 62 billion euros, which would increase Finland's GDP by 40 per cent.³⁵ In England, the number was £1.24 trillion, about 60 per cent of England's GDP.³⁶ These numbers give us a sense of the scope of this work, and this is important. But they don't tell us much about long-term value creation. They are as useful as saying that a heath is less valuable than a forest. Neither tells us that care work and nature are the bedrocks of the market, not just part of it.

GDP (and therefore the established economy) tends to use prices to 'split' things up. Nature is divided into products, and society is divided into individuals. The individual parts are priced as if they were independent of one another. This makes it very difficult from an economic perspective to account for relational value creation, for example when a larger mushroom helps a smaller one. The mushrooms create something together that neither of them would have been able to alone. The little mushroom would never have become great and fat without the other. But if you give them individual prices, that value and that work disappears. The same is true of people who provide care, both for pay and without it.

Even more importantly, in GDP less wild nature and fewer unpaid hours spent with those we love will always look like we got richer. We can't see what we lose when we lose something priceless.

In 2024, a group of economists were surprised to discover that the financial crisis of 2008, which had left millions unemployed, extended the average life expectancy of Americans. The impact was greatest among the least educated. The researchers wrote that 'economic activity' in general increased excessive mortality, particularly because of the amount of pollution associated with these activities.[37] Established economics, which does not take the maintenance of human beings and the planet into account, can result in a system in which an increasing amount of economic activity, or what we call growth, can in fact shorten our lives. In which crises literally make it easier to breathe. In which the things that give us money also kill us, making our lives poorer, shorter, more brutish.

LOSING SOLUTIONS

The perception that priceless things are worthless influences political decision-making. Many see gender inequality on the labour market and blame it on women's 'economic inactivity'. The global consulting firm McKinsey estimated that if women were as active in business as men, global GDP would increase by $28 trillion.[38] They called it a 'full potential' scenario. Hurrah! The assumption is that what women do outside of the labour market wouldn't be missed by society. As I mentioned in the introduction, 708 million women worldwide say that they are not in paid work because of care responsibilities.

Across the globe, many more women work part time than men. In England, for example, 87 per cent of men in the workforce work full time, while the same is true for only 59 per cent of women.[39] In the entire eurozone, 28 per cent of women work part time, while only 8 per cent of men do.[40] Like McKinsey, many economists see part-time work as a waste of women's working potential, and this has major consequences for women's income over their lives. For this reason, the Danish regional authority recommended in 2022 that more women working in the healthcare sector transition from part- to full-time work. They needed more hands. The recommendation briefly alluded to the problem of scheduling, but there was otherwise no mention of families or household work, which has a significant impact – women with one child in Denmark are twice as likely to work part time as those without any children. This is particularly true of jobs that require one to be physically present, and often at night: '60% of female social workers go part time for 5 years after having their first child, while 41% of female nurses, 28% of female teachers and 45% of female care workers go part time.'[41] In the UK, census data shows that having children also has drastic consequences for working parents: 'More than half of families with only one child had both parents working full-time, compared with 39.5% of families with three or more children.'[42]

It is true that women don't work as much as men if you look only at individuals and their paid work, as many economic analyses tend to. But if you grab your feminist magnifying glass and see the family as a unit and add invisible, unpaid household work to the equation, you will see a different picture. *No one* on the labour market is an isolated individual.

Feminism has been enormously successful in campaigning for women's right to stay in the workforce after having children (the welfare state plays a significant role here, as we'll see later on). All over the world, women's paid employment has increased over the past 50 years. This is completely essential to the personal freedom women have to live, work, and love as they please. A woman without a salary or with a significantly lower salary than their partner is in a very vulnerable position, and you don't have to look that far back into the past to see the link between economic dependence and stifling oppression.

But this high employment rate can also make it an ordeal to have children. The economic freedom that is so essential for women to lead dignified lives has made life's other joys more difficult to participate in.

Denmark has been remarkably successful in getting women into paid work. In 2023 The Economic Council of the Labour Movement published a report showing that, 'In Danish families, parents work 27 hours per week on average. This is more than the EU countries we normally compare ourselves to.'[43] The UK presents similar numbers. While women with no children on average work 40 hours a week, as soon as the child is born, this drops sharply to just below 30. Men's paid labour time hardly changes at all.[44] In Denmark, mothers and fathers work roughly the same number of hours every day if you add paid and unpaid work together. In the UK, women actually work 12 minutes more than men every day, if we're being exact.[45] This ought to put those lofty ambitions for more women to work full time in a new light. What exactly should they stop doing in order to have more time to work?

In January 2023, a chief economist from the Danish Confederation of Employers wrote:

> Just before Christmas, Danish Bureau of Statistics released new reports that showed that city and regional employees have a significantly higher percentage of sick leave compared to private sector employees. In 2021, full time workers in the municipalities and regions took 14.5 and 13.6 days of sick leave respectively as a result of their own illnesses. By contrast, in the private sector, the average was 7.4 days.
>
> The high rate of sick leave in the public sector results in a significant loss of work

potential. If sick leave for public sector employees was on par with that of private employees in similar job roles, this would correspond to approximately 8,200 more full time employees, and 5,700 full time employees in the municipal offices.[46]

We need to put our feminist detective hats on to analyse claims like these. When economics doesn't offer any useful methods to measure the care needs of a family, you need to put the pieces together yourself. The chief economists' statistics seem so simple: objective and straightforward. But paid work does not occur in a vacuum. So, let's take a closer look at the care context of work. What kinds of activities underlie something as simple as a sick day in Denmark? Most public sector workers in municipalities and regions are women. In municipalities 77 per cent of employees are women, and in regions 78 per cent. But why would women be sick more often than men?[47] There are multiple reasons, but let's start in one corner of their unpaid work: sick kids.

Sick kids are an invisible force shaping women's working lives. In the UK, the official statistics also show that 36 per cent of women took sick leave from work, as opposed to only 28 per cent of men.[48] However, when these numbers were researched more thoroughly by analysts, it became clear that it wasn't the women who were sick, it was their children. Due to the often rigid rules around paid sick leave, many parents will lie and say that they themselves are ill.[49] Even in Denmark, where many have the right to be paid to stay at home with an ill child, people lie: in 2021, a survey from Epinion in Denmark found that 68 per cent of parents who responded said that they had little to no choice to stay home with their kids when they were sick, and half said that they sometimes needed to lie and say that they themselves were ill.[50] In America, it was found in 2014 that women were a staggering ten times as likely to stay home with an ill child than men. Mothers were also five times as likely to take their children to doctor's appointments.[51]

The sick child presents a double bind for women, as they are not only overrepresented in care work at home, but also in the paid care work demanded by the rest of society.[52] This puts women in an incredibly difficult situation, as their absence from work and their absence from home can both have severe health and well-being consequences for other people.[53] In 2020, when the COVID-19 pandemic hit, it became clear that not everyone can work from home. In the United States, more women than men were employed in 'essential' jobs.[54] Every third woman, in fact. Up to 90 per cent of those employed in the healthcare sector globally, the so-called front-line workers, who were in direct contact with patients, were women, according to the *Lancet*.[55] Like many other care tasks, these jobs required employees to be physically present to do their work.

Those working in higher up positions or in the private sector often have more flexibility, which means that they, for example, can work from home. Women are often subject to the fact that they, both outside of and in the home, do work that is time-sensitive and cannot be postponed, and requires them to be in a specific place. This puts them at risk of needing to call in sick so they can take care of their kids.

If we take as an example a couple where one person works in the private sector and the other in the public sector, it will usually be the care worker (or the one with the lower salary) who looks like they are 'constantly sick' because working from home isn't a possibility for them. If the couple has a gendered dynamic, in which the woman has more care responsibilities, then she will be more likely to look like she takes more sick leave.

Taking care of sick children is just one example of something that needs to be done but cannot be prioritised or included in political discussions because it is impossible to systematically include in the day-today running of an economy. Our working lives are structured as if children do not get sick, despite the fact that sickness is a near constant for young children, and *should* be, because their immune systems are developing. In the Danish magazine *Samvirke*, a paediatrician at Rigshospitalet estimates that during the first two years of their lives, children are typically sick three to seven days per month. Twenty to 30 per cent of children are sick even more frequently. This corresponds roughly to 60 sick days per year for the first two years of a child's life. Up until they are six years old, children are sick about once a month.[56] A study of the Netherlands, Canada and England showed that only 65 per cent of men think that their managers see men as active caregivers in their families.[57] It is simply assumed, by many, that these sick days do not exist for many male workers.

In her article 'Nobody Knows', Rebecca Solnit writes that we often say that knowledge is power but forget that the ability to ignore what is happening is also a sign of power: 'The powerful swathe themselves in obliviousness in order to avoid the pain of others ... the more you are, the less you know.'[58]

Established economics relies on the notion of the 'normal worker', who is isolated from their surroundings. Everyone should strive to be the men whose work life doesn't change when they have children. They are, apparently, the ones creating actual value, while those not in paid work 'sponge' and create nothing. In this view, it looks like the parent who is 'sick' or working part time is creating a deficit for society. But maybe they are creating a surplus for a new citizen. We have no idea whether a woman calling in sick to care for a sick child is creating or subtracting value. But in current political debates there is no doubt: we would be richer if women lived more like men. This statement glosses over the reality of what the home creates in the economy.

PAID TO PATCH UP YOUR BOYFRIEND'S EGO

Before we continue on established economics' journey all the way into the uterus, I'd like to revisit a historical movement.

In 1972, Mariarosa Dalla Costa, Silvia Federici, Brigitte Galtier and Selma James, all feminists from the Global North, started the Wages for Housework (WfH) movement. Their thinking was rooted in Dalla Costa's experiences from the Italian workers' movement, where she noticed that women's oppression on the labour market took a different form than her male colleagues. WfH asked: what really creates economic value?

Their answer was radical, both then and now: work that takes place in the home creates value, and the construction of the family is a matter of economics rather than nature, God or mushrooms: 'They say it is love. We say it is unwaged work.'[59]

They said that the housewife had been subject to super-exploitation.[60] There were three layers of society that extracted value from her without her seeing a penny. Her unwaged work enabled, first, her husband's income; second, his boss; and thirdly, it was the source of new workers for society. In one particularly memorable sentence, Silvia Federici wrote that a woman works for her husband by 'patch[ing] up his ego when it is crushed by the work and the social relations ... that capital has reserved for him.'[61] The home is where you escape to become a whole human in a world where you are treated like a product. Can anyone else relate?

Women, in other words, weren't just creating new workers through childbirth and child rearing. They were maintaining the existing workforce by providing emotional labour, making dinner, and so on.

For me, the main takeaway from WfH is that it showed us that unpaid, reproductive work is an essential economic activity and a skillset that requires specialised knowledge. When domestic tasks are reduced to being seen as 'natural' or 'unproductive', as they have been by large swathes of economics up until now, this obscures the fact that housework is also 'working' for those who make a profit. The gender roles that constitute the nuclear family are not biological. They are economic.

The naturalisation of the home has contributed to the isolation of the mother that has dominated Western culture since the Enlightenment. Because the home has been represented as a space external to civilisation and rationality, society has failed to acknowledge the fact that it is enormously difficult to look after other people. Today, wealthy parents can pay for lactation consultants and birth preparation classes and spend infinite hours browsing the finest newborn gear. But that doesn't change the fact that many experts consider the closed-off nuclear family a suboptimal way of rearing children.

Rebecca Sear, professor of anthropology and behavioural evolution at Brunel University in London, has suggested that, because so much of the social sciences is based on the Western middle-class family, there is a risk of 'naturalising' the idea of the nuclear family as something biologically fated. However, she says: 'evidence from disciplines that take a cross-cultural or historical perspective shows that in most human societies, multiple individuals beyond the mother are typically involved in raising children: in evolutionary anthropology, it is now widely accepted that we have evolved a strategy of cooperative reproduction.'[62]

The reproduction of people, in its broadest sense, requires skills and a strong community from the outset. Being pregnant and giving birth without adequate resources can be fatal. Worldwide 290,000 women die from this every year.[63] In the United States the number of maternal deaths has doubled in the past two decades.[64] And once you have given birth, you don't just hold the baby to your chest to feed it. Breastfeeding is a skill that requires practice. Not to mention all of the tasks that come with the following years, both physically and psychologically. Sear concludes: 'Expecting mothers to care for children with little support, while expecting fathers to provide for their families with little support, is, therefore, likely to lead to adverse health consequences for mothers, fathers and children.' In Germany, 71 per cent of couples are equal in terms of work before their first child is born. After the child is born, this is only true of 15 per cent of relationships. Fifty-five per cent of women work fewer hours as a result. Seventeen per cent stop working entirely.[65]

All political decisions affect our families: housing, taxes, tariffs, workers' rights. But in the language of much of economics, the home is treated like a black box, a private matter.

When the economic system is organised as it is, the person with the lowest salary will usually be the one who ends up being the primary caretaker. This is the cheapest option for the family, and it is assumed to be the cheapest option for society, because that person's time is worth the least. Gender roles are a division of labour.

This was why WfH called for wages for housework. Not to put a price on housework but rather to show that this work requires time, resources and respect. The home is not just a private space. Those who make a profit from its labours need to help turn it into a dignified and meaningful place to be.

THE STATE'S CHEAP KIDS

As we have by now established, an incredible amount of value creation takes place in the home, even though what takes place here is often seen as 'a deficit' – and as something that women in particular should distance themselves from so that they can play a more active role in the labour market.

I am writing this in 2024, when media outlets all over the world are terribly worried about declining fertility rates.[66] Denmark's politicians and major think tanks are shaking in their boots over the projected dearth of future workers. And what has happened? The Danish prime minister suggested in her New Year's Address that the state could subsidise fertility treatment for a second child.[67] This immediately came on the tail of the removal of a time limitation of how long a woman's eggs could be frozen.[68] And soon after, the government decided to propose legislation that would allow partner egg donation, a form of fertility treatment in which a woman can donate an egg to her female partner so she can carry the pregnancy.[69] After decades during which LGBTQIA+ people have been accused of being dangerous to children, 'not real families' and the like, there is now a rush to 'naturalise' the queer family when it is a matter of increasing the potential workforce. What counts as an accepted family structure is usually related to a society's economic needs.

Don't get me wrong: there is no problem with these proposals. It is wonderful that people who want to have children can. But there is no reason to believe that the state is doing this for their sake. This is an economic calculus that directly contradicts the rhetoric that families often receive: that having children is a 'private' matter, and that it's your problem if your daily life doesn't work, or if there are cuts to public childcare and healthcare. The state wants children, but it wants them to be cheap. When people complain that their taxes are going to 'other people's children', we could tell them that 'other people's children' are their own future employees. Any parent could flip this argument and complain: the fruits of my unpaid care work are being monetised by employers and I don't get a dime. As always, value can be shuffled around.

In 2016, Italy introduced a new national holiday: 22 September would henceforth be known as 'Fertility Day'. Driven by fears of a declining population, the state posted memes, including one that depicted a pregnant woman holding out her hand. In her hand was an hourglass. It said: 'Beauty doesn't have an age. Fertility does.'[70] My favourite part of the campaign, however, was a picture of an older man, which read, 'When I was your age, I had three kids, and I lost one testicle in the war – #fertilityday.' I don't think the meme with the woman was necessary; I doubt many women are unaware of society's ideas about what makes a woman's life a source of pride or shame. We have all heard the horror stories of those poor childless women, the 'cat ladies', and seen the patronising looks. Anecdotally, it has been my experience that whenever a person expresses regret at not being able to have children, they are never asked why. It is seen as an entirely understandable and universal desire that doesn't require explanation. But when a person expresses that they are happily childless, the question is always 'Why?!' This form of social control serves a political function: more children.

Cultural narratives don't always correspond to reality. In 2019, a British researcher found that the happiest people in the United Kingdom and the United States were unmarried women without children.[71] He pointed out, moreover, that what occasionally made these women unhappy was not their lives but rather the stigmas they encountered. Married men lived longer lives and were happier than single men, but the opposite was true of women. There is no doubt that parenthood can be a great source of joy. But this is not a given, and for many people the opposite can be wonderful too.[72]

Our family patterns and divisions of labour are not just a private matter. When we use metrics like GDP, it becomes difficult to transfer time and resources to areas that are seen as worthless. It will always be interpreted as a loss, both for the individual and society, when we spend more time on unpaid care. But this doesn't mean that value does not exist outside of GDP. There is a constant economic need for new, functioning, healthy workers, but the established economic calculus sees the time spent doing precisely this as a loss. Everyone earns money from this unpaid labour except the people who provide it.

POWER STRUGGLES

'The true focus of revolutionary change is never merely the oppressive situations which we seek to escape, but that piece of the oppressor which is planted deep within each of us, and which knows only the oppressors' tactics, the oppressors' relationships.'

AUDRE LORDE, *SISTER OUTSIDER*

CHAPTER 6

When I was a child, I loved eating the heel of a loaf of bread. My father did too. Every Sunday morning, he grabbed the end piece and said with a smile, 'You'll just have to wait until you become a father.'

Many women have striven to become the celebrated 'normal' productive person – the father – who creates an economic surplus, gaining recognition and economic independence along the way. Since early feminism, we have debated whether this is possible or even desirable. The lines were drawn early, and they remain the same today. What does freedom look like, and who has the right to it?

The version of freedom represented by *Homo economicus* is, according to the philosopher Seyla Benhabib, conditioned by invisible care, as we explored in chapter 3. This invisibility is necessary to maintain the fantasy that one is not dependent on other human beings. We saw this in the calculation of women working part time. Many 'normal' fathers are only able to work full time because there is invisible work taking place behind the scenes.

This dynamic, in which one person is 'free' and the other is 'oppressed', exists in many parts of our society and many activists and thinkers have seen it as one of the most defining dynamics of Western culture.

In *Refugees from Amerika: A Gay Manifesto* (1970), the activist Carl Wittman wrote about the way heterosexual society – with one independent person and one caregiver – is entrenched in the entire organisation of the economy and work: 'One of the worst of straight concepts is inequality. Straight (also white, English, male, capitalist) thinking views things in terms of order and comparison. A is before B, B is after A; one is below two is below three; there is no room for equality. This idea gets extended to male/female, on top/on bottom, spouse/not spouse, heterosexual/homosexual; boss/worker, white/black and rich/poor ... *stop mimicking straights, stop censoring ourselves.*'[1] Wittman challenges the idea that everyone can become an A, that everyone can be on top.

Some people are able to present themselves as independent because they take the care they receive for granted. To see oneself as independent is the same as having power. To strive for this ideal of freedom is therefore the same as striving for power over other people. If you think that you don't need care, this is only because you don't see the care you receive. We cannot be a society of fathers.

< >

Middle- and upper-class women who were married with children started to be in greater demand in the workplace during the period of economic prosperity that followed in the decades after the Second World War. This ushered in a new era for feminism because it seemed to offer a new opportunity for more autonomy and an identity outside the home. The labour market became synonymous with freedom.

In her book *The Feminine Mystique*, published in 1963, the feminist Betty Friedan launched what would come to be called second wave feminism. The activist and professor bell hooks describes her experience of the second wave in her book *Feminist Theory* (1984): 'As feminist movements progressed, critiques of the notion of power as domination and control were submerged as bourgeois activists began to focus on women overcoming their fear of power (the implication being that if they wanted social equality with men, they would need to participate equally in exercising domination and control over others.)'[2] The brand of feminism launched by Friedan has probably had more influence than any other kind of feminism. It made a few heel pieces of bread available to a select group of women.

The historian Susan Ferguson explains in her book *Women and Work* that Betty Friedan became the standard bearer of a line of thinking focused on the sexist culture of society and women's own self-image and psychological well-being.[3] Friedan's main character is the white middle-class American housewife. She coined the phrase 'the problem with no name' to describe the inner emptiness that hangs like a cloud over 'the perfect housewives', who have a house, a dog and a husband but are still deeply depressed. Friedan challenges these women to understand that through advertising and cultural norms, they have been falsely led to believe that this is a worthwhile life and that they don't belong in the workplace. The shame of not being a good mother because you want to actualise yourself outside the home permeates the whole book, and it is this shame that Friedan challenges women to overcome.

In the 1950s and 1960s, the mental health of white American middle-class women was in such a dire state that doctors began prescribing sedatives on a mass scale. Doctors had columns in women's magazines, where mothers could write in with their problems, which were usually just barely veiled howls of existential despair. The doctor would then recommend a prescription. The medicine – often Valium – was called 'Mother's Little Helper'.[4]

Friedan shed light on a serious issue: white, middle-class women's deep sense of unhappiness in their roles as housewives. But she did not address the economic conditions that underpinned this unhappiness, or the fates of men. In the Friedan narrative, fathers appeared to be free, powerful and happy, living the ideal life.

Instead, she emphasised the psychological and interpersonal problems of women's oppression, particularly discrimination and the extremely degrading treatment women faced at home and in the workplace. To solve these problems, Friedan argued that women needed to abandon 'the feminine mystique' (the sexism that permeated their minds) and be empowered to demand what was theirs. A precursor to today's 'Girlboss' and *Lean In*-feminism, the primary obstacle in *The Feminine Mystique* was women's own self-image and the sexist opinions and behaviour of a few men.

The book was massively influential. But from the start, it was clear that something was off. One of the most prominent historians of gender in the United States, Gerda Lerner, wrote a letter to Friedan in which she congratulated her on the book, which she found 'splendid' and interesting. But she also felt compelled to state:

> you address yourself solely to the problems of middle-class, college-educated women. This approach was one of the shortcomings of the suffrage movement for many years and has, I believe, retarded the general advance of women. Working women, especially Negro women, labour not only under the disadvantages imposed by the feminine mystique, but under the more pressing disadvantages of economic discrimination. To leave them out of consideration of the problem or to ignore the contributions they can make toward its solution, is something we simply cannot afford to do.[5,6]

Friedan's focus should provoke reflection, even today. Some people might recognise this brand of feminism from Greta Gerwig's *Barbie* movie. This feminism understands women as brainwashed by a patriarchy that they need to 'wake up' from and confront head on. The primary evil of patriarchy is that it has tricked women into thinking that they are not clever enough to work. In the film, the nearly hypnotised Barbies are packed into the back of a truck where they are given a speech about, among other things, the unjust double standards that women face. When they tumble out of the truck, there is in reality nothing preventing their liberation. No violence, no poverty, no oppression. An ungenerous reading would be that patriarchy only continues to exist because women are too dumb to realise it. In *Barbie*, oppression is basically just in our heads. Barbie's slogan for many years was: 'If you can dream it, you can be it.' This is actually a pretty accurate summary of economics' mechanical human without a past, culture or structural barriers.

Friedan wrote articles in the newspaper about America's poorest women and the economic aspects of their oppression, so she was well acquainted with the fates of the women she neglected to write about. Gerda Lerner's letter cannot possibly have come as a surprise. Friedan chose the feminism that aligned best with the reigning world view.

THE EMPIRE STRIKES BACK

Feminist agendas do not exist in an economic vacuum – there are interests that pull us in various directions. And there are certain agendas that have had an easier time breaking through, as is still the case today.

The years surrounding the publication of *The Feminine Mystique* were characterised by extreme anti-communism in the United States, a phenomenon we know as 'the Red Scare'. Two senators founded the

House Un-American Activities Committee (HUAC) and held live hearings that were broadcast on national television, in which every person and their mother were accused of being communists if they had come into the slightest contact with trade unions, left-wing beliefs or mentioned Karl Marx in a bar. The accused could sometimes save themselves by ratting others out. If you refused to respond to questioning, you were thrown in jail. The accused included everyone from secretaries employed by the federal government to some of the most famous artists in the country. The fear of communism was used to undermine many of the civil rights movements of the time. Martin Luther King's economic theories and collaborations with communists were used to justify the constant FBI surveillance he was subject to during his most productive and influential years of activism.[7]

The Red Scare influenced economic power struggles as well. During this period, attacks were made on alternative economic analyses, and resources were funnelled into establishing a particular interpretation of value, wages and justice.

In the 1930s, the American president Franklin D. Roosevelt introduced the New Deal, which was based on the established economics of its time: that the market should be regulated and that the state had a key role to play in education, healthcare and fair working conditions. These new policies included, among other things, unemployment benefits, better options for union organising and reduced work hours. Many of these policies remain in place in the Scandinavian countries today. But in the United States, many of these ideas were vehemently opposed and lobbied against after the adoption of the New Deal, which increased tax rates to 75 per cent for those earning over a million dollars a year. The rich weren't particularly happy about that.

In the 1940s, the titans of American industry worked actively to remove the economist Lorie Tarshis' textbook, *Elements of Economics*, from American universities because it was based on the theories of John Maynard Keynes. Some of the largest American companies paid 'activists' to send thousands of complaint letters to American universities that were using the book. These letters claimed that Tarshis was preaching communist propaganda, trying to deprive Americans of their freedom and – horror of horrors – turn the United States into a socialist country like England.

Six months later, Tarshis' book was blacklisted and replaced by a book by Paul Samuelson. Samuelson's brand of economic thinking claimed to combine Keynesian ideas with marginalist microeconomics in a 'neoclassical synthesis'. The role of the state here was more ambiguous, and the role of reproductive work outside and inside the home was relegated to the background.[8] For Samuelson, the market would reach equilibrium in the long run, and prices were a good indicator of value. Keynes would joke about this type of economics and say: 'In the long run we are all dead.' But Samuelson's ideas won the fight and even he later admitted in a private letter that he called his theory the 'neoclassical synthesis' so that he could escape the searchlight of the Red Scare. Even minor elements of Keynes' ideas posed a threat to one's personal safety.[9]

The journalist Zachary Carter writes in his book about Keynes: 'Where Tarshis had issued a warning about the limits of the market in a democracy, Samuelson revived the power of the market to order social preferences, with the help of just a little fiscal adjustment.'[10] Ideas about care and equality that had been so successful in Europe were fought tooth and nail in the United States. This power struggle is still happening today. In 2014, the *Huffington Post* revealed that the Koch brothers, two of America's richest men, poured money into economic teaching and research with the aim of demonstrating the supremacy of the market when it came to distributing wealth, starting with kids still in high school.[11]

When Paul Samuelson claimed that he would rather write a country's economic textbooks than its laws, it was probably with the knowledge that he had been allowed to write those textbooks because his view of economics wouldn't create any trouble for those who held the most power in American society. He made economic inequality look like the result of a natural law that shouldn't be meddled with.

The story of Tarshis, Samuelson and the Koch brothers shows us just how dangerous it is to see economics as a neutral science. Economics can be used to safeguard special interests without anyone realising. This is not necessarily the fault of economists. But it does mean that we need to keep a watchful eye on economic statements, analyses and judgements. Political agendas can be hidden in what appear to be objective calculations.

BETTY'S MAIDS

In her letter to Betty Friedan, Gerda Lerner repeated what many Black feminists had been saying for a long time. In the book *Ain't I a Woman?* (1981) bell hooks examined the women's rights movements from the perspective of Black women. She recounts pervasive racism and a lack of solidarity across races.

For many white middle-class women, focusing on their own presence on the labour market was intentional. hooks writes: 'It was not in the opportunistic interests of white middle- and upper-class participants in the women's movement to draw attention to the plight of poor women, or the specific plight of Black women. A white woman professor who wants the public to see her as victimized and oppressed because she is denied tenure is not about to evoke images of poor women working as domestics receiving less than the minimum wage struggling to raise a family single-handed.'[12]

Feminism that only addresses the problems that affect the groups that are closest to power has an explicit interest in denying space to less privileged women. For someone in power, giving the most privileged women access to what the most privileged men already have is far easier than challenging the entire way the market assesses and distributes resources. For that reason, the most privileged women in the United States were also guilty of obscuring care and its value in the economy. In an almost grotesque replay of the problem with Adam Smith's mother, it transpired that Betty Friedan had hired help so that she could work full time as a journalist.[13] Like Smith, she didn't recognise the value of the people making her dinner, taking care of her children or mopping her floors either.

An hour before writing these lines, I read that the Danish government has just agreed that Filipino and Indian care workers should be brought to Denmark to do the jobs that Danes don't want to do anymore because the conditions and pay are so poor. This is a geopolitical version of Adam Smith's mother. Some women free themselves from needing to perform badly paid care. But this doesn't make the need for care disappear. It just means we need to recruit a new class of people with even less agency to work for less than they are worth.[14]

THE RIGHT NOT TO LOSE

The dominant form of feminism that followed *The Feminine Mystique* illustrates hooks' point. It bears traces of Friedan's limited purview. It led to a focus on legal rights, such as the right not to be discriminated against or harassed in the workplace. These struggles shouldn't be dismissed. They are, of course, a cornerstone of every society that prioritises civil rights. The #MeToo movement showed that fundamental rights to participate in the public sphere remain badly suppressed every day and everywhere. But as Nancy Fraser writes in her book *Fortunes of Feminism*, legal equality is not sufficient to create a society in which all lives are valued. Among men, legal equality exists. This doesn't mean that there aren't men suffering horrific fates that could have been avoided in a more caring society.

This discussion has occasionally divided feminism in two. The marketplace sociologist Paula England outlines the camps. The first 'emphasises the exclusion of women from traditionally male activities and institutions. For example, laws, cultural beliefs, and other discriminatory practices that have excluded most women from politics, religious leadership, military positions, and traditionally male crafts and professions within paid employment.' This is the feminism we recognise from *Barbie* and Betty Friedan. But there is also another kind of feminism, the one this book argues for, which 'emphasises the devaluation of and low material rewards accorded to activities and traits that traditionally have been deemed appropriate for women. The sexism here is in failing to see how much traditionally female activities or dispositions contribute to the economy, society, or polity ... Feminists who emphasise this sort of sexism see the remedy to include changing values that deprecate traditionally female activities as well as allocating higher rewards to such activities.'[15]

Some people feel that there is an unbreakable conflict between these two positions, but I don't agree. There is nothing in the second position that excludes the possibility of engaging in the first. On the contrary, they can work together. In my view, a greater appreciation of care is the only way that we can achieve economic equality in paid work. But if you exclusively deal with the first position, you can end up perpetuating the shame and lack of appreciation associated with traditionally female activities. Then you end up with a kind of feminism in which no privileged individuals, of any gender, care to perform any care.

As the political theorists Cinzia Arruzza, Nancy Fraser and Tithi Bhattacharya write in *Feminism for the 99%*: 'We have no interest in breaking the glass ceiling while leaving the vast majority to clean up the shards.'[16]

Friedan succeeded in showing us that all kinds of people have the right to compete on equal footing to win in society. And this isn't nothing! But she didn't show us that no one deserves to lose.

AIN'T I A WOMAN?

Both Betty Friedan and the Wages for Housework movement were criticised for putting way too much focus on unwaged housework and too little on the fact that care, for many of society's poorest women, since time immemorial, has been paid work that they did for other people, which took time away from their own nearest and dearest. For many marginalised women, access to the marketplace was not synonymous with freedom; they had been paid for a long time, and freedom was yet to appear.

Two critiques in particular have grown out of the debate about paid care work: firstly, that unpaid care is not always oppressive, and secondly, that wealthy women's liberation should not come at the expense of women from lower social and economic classes.

Feminism's task became to combine the analyses of paid and unpaid work, such that their contexts could be understood and used to create solidarity across class and race. Angela Davis succeeded in doing so in her book *Women, Race and Class*. The case of racism in the United States is unique because of the country's extremely late abolition of slavery, but Davis' thinking can also be used to understand the struggle for more care today outside the United States. Her work abandons the attempt to describe a universal, female experience, and instead focuses on what characterises all care activities in the dominant global economic system. And so she gives voice to very different women's understandings of freedom and their experiences of exploitation and oppression.

Betty Friedan described her job as a journalist as self-actualising and identity-creating, whereas the family was the place in which her identity was limited. But the strenuous physical labour that many Black women have undertaken was not necessarily 'self-actualising'. They mostly worked these jobs because they needed the money.

In the 1960s, a third of all Black women in the United States worked in care-related jobs, often in white families and with white people's children, so that the white mother could see to more refined household duties or maybe even make a little money of her own (homes in the United States in the 1960s really excelled in crafting various types and levels of female oppression).[17] The so-called *domestics* that white families hired to work in their homes usually only saw their own children every second or third week. They couldn't afford to see them more often. Black women were cheap labour because they were – and still are – systematically discriminated against in the labour market. Their lives looked radically different from the middle-class life of the suburbs. Their perspective on family was therefore also completely different. Domestics fought for the right to spend time with their children, not for the right to get away from them. Both paid work and unpaid care are privileges and burdens.[18]

For women who experienced racism, discrimination and possibly tough working environments, the family represented a refuge where they could escape the oppressive structures that dominated their lives and paid work. The home is a place in which you both resist the power of the market and simultaneously create value for those who hold that power. It is a fundamentally paradoxical space.

And this remains true today. As Elizabeth Martinez wrote in 1998 in her book *De Colores Means All of Us*: 'The family is also seen differently by women from the colonial experience. It often serves as a fortress, a defense against the inimical forces of the dominant society, a source of strength for a people whose identity is constantly under attack.'[19]

Davis argued that the home was one of the only places where Black women in the United States had real agency. Because the dominant form of feminism exclusively saw the home as an oppressive prison, it occluded the reality that for many women – as well as many of the most vulnerable men – working ruthless, poorly paid jobs was hell. And it overlooked that the struggle for the right to work might have ended up in an exciting place for the most fortunate women, just as it did for the most fortunate men, but for many, many people, waged work was something to fight against, not for.[20]

Betty Friedan believed that if you were 'satisfied' by staying at home, then you were deluding yourself. This was not the case for those who used their homes to foster and protect their communities. The role of the home still looms large in feminism today. The writer Gabriella Beckles-Raymond describes this balance between being outside and inside the home as part of the British–Caribbean minority in England in 2020: 'We challenge the private/public distinction by using our homes in communal, social and political ways; rejecting the excessive urge to keep others out, while simultaneously giving our own bodies the privacy, regard and love so often withheld or denied by others.'[21] These feminists see a completely different potential in the family and the home, precisely because the home is one of the last places left where the market doesn't preside over each hour.

When I hear women say that they envy men, I often think: be careful what you wish for. In Denmark today, as we have seen, men's work hours remain largely unchanged when they have children. In 2021, during a debate about parental leave, one father wrote in the Danish magazine *Femina* that he only had two weeks of leave to spend with his daughters due to economic pressures on his family. He called it his biggest regret, and said that: 'The consequence today is that I sometimes feel that I am watching my family from the sidelines instead of being at its core ... And once you've had that experience it is easy to slide further and further away from your family and that feeling of alienation and take refuge in the secure and practical haven of work.'[22] It is tough to be pushed into the home because of economic reasons. But it is also tough to be pushed out of it for economic reasons. It is often said that women perform more care work than men. This is of course true at face value. But in my experience many men see their paid work as caring for their family: making sure there is food on the table, new sneakers, maybe a vacation. They are motivated to work by love, too. But it is a love that expresses itself quite distantly from those who receive it. If we reduce men's motivations to work to 'self-interest', I think we are missing an important piece of the puzzle: that love and family play a huge role in the labour market, not only for women, but also for men.

In a pamphlet from 1971, Selma James and Mariarosa Dalla Costa from WfH write: 'Now it is clear that not one of us believes that emancipation, liberation, can be achieved through work … Those who advocate that the liberation of the working class woman lies in her getting a job outside the home are part of the problem, not the solution.'[23] The struggle for autonomy, freedom and one's own income shouldn't slip into an idealisation of the marketplace and an escape from everything in our lives that is difficult to value.

If you make this mistake, you can easily forget about all the people who are denied the possibility to provide unwaged care. A contemporary example in Denmark is the so-called 'ghetto law', which has targeted residents of certain neighbourhoods that meet a number of criteria, including unemployment levels, local criminality and rates of inhabitants of 'non-Western' ethnicity. Since 2019, children in these so-called 'ghettos' have been forced to start in the public daycare system when they are only one year old – a choice which is otherwise up to parents and is usually based on the individual child's development and private household concerns.[24] Daycare, which is normally presented as an essential tool to secure women's equality in paid work, is in this case used to deprive poor, immigrant citizens of the right to provide unwaged care work for their own children to the extent that they would like.

The ghetto law's way of regulating who gets to spend time with their children is a continuation of a long and brutal history. In Denmark, Greenlandic children in the 1950s were forcibly removed from their parents and brought to Denmark to be 're-educated'. This form of state intervention against marginalised people's right to provide unwaged care has many parallels across the world, particularly with regards to

Indigenous peoples, first nations, minorities and other socio-economically vulnerable populations.[25]

A similar dynamic can be seen in discussions about the right to access abortions. Feminism has, rightly, focused on securing this right. It is a struggle for the right not to provide care when you cannot or do not want to, and it remains an essential fight for freedom and autonomy. But we have often overlooked just how many people have been denied the right to have a child, even though they wanted to. Until the 1970s, Denmark forced Greenlandic women to have IUDs without their consent, and in Canada, Indigenous women were sterilised without their consent.[26] Politics doesn't only shape who we think has the right to receive care. It also shapes our views about who has the right to provide it.

The most vulnerable women, including migrants, sex workers, refugees and women in the lowest paid jobs, in which work is a matter of survival, struggle *to be able to* provide unwaged care alongside participating equally in the marketplace. The Filipino and Indian care workers who will be brought to Denmark will also miss and be missed by their local friends, families and welfare states.

The fight for a more caring society requires a break with the feminism that takes the position of men as the measuring stick for liberation. If we don't see value in the activities that have traditionally been associated with femininity, the poorest paid and most vulnerable people will be gravely impacted. These are the people who have the toughest time buying and fighting for more time, peace and closeness with their loved ones, because their bodies and time are the least valued.

A CONSTRUCTED WOMAN

Angela Davis' main insight in *Women, Race and Class* was that those who have power in the marketplace will try to make care as cheap as possible. Legislation, economic incentives, migration, violence and cultural socialisation on the basis of gender can be used to that end. What a 'woman' is can be adapted to the kind of work that society needs her to do at any given point in time. Davis writes, for example, about women under slavery: 'But women suffered in different ways as well … Expediency governed the slaveholders' posture toward female slaves: when it was profitable to exploit them as if they were men, they were regarded, in effect, as genderless, but when they could be exploited, punished and repressed in ways suited only for women, they were locked in their exclusively female roles.'[27]

For future care workers that will come to Denmark from India and the Philippines, you can see this adaptation taking place in a very concrete way. These people will go from being denied residency in the country to suddenly being welcomed, if they are willing to provide a particular kind of service cheaply. If they want to play a – historically gendered – role in society, they are welcome. If not, they are not. The Brown woman is an eternally flexible figure in the Western imagination, and with the stroke of a pen, she can go from being an economic burden or threatening migrant to a desirable caretaker.

< >

In Europe in the 1950s, just as in the United States, sexism against the middle-class woman was shaped by the perception of her stupidity and superficiality, but also her caring nature, which made her well-suited to undertake free work in the home as well as poorly paid jobs as nurses or the like.

In the 1960s and 1970s women in Denmark went from making up 26 per cent of the paid workforce to 44 per cent.[28] The historian Anette Borchorst writes that many welfare reforms in the 1960s in Denmark were primarily structured to get women into the workforce. Denmark needed what she calls a 'double breadwinner model'. This meant that unpaid care was deprioritised to escalate paid care. A similar phenomenon happened in the rest of the Western world, but the Scandinavian welfare states have taken this process much further. She calls it 'defamiliarisation'.[29] There was an alliance between feminism and the priorities of established economics: now everyone would be a daddy, and GDP would grow. The normal worker who works eight hours, rests eight hours and sleeps eight hours would now be genderless. Women would have more freedom, their own money. And there would be all kinds of new cultural narratives about her.

Introducing: the multitasking woman! Women, who were previously seen as being intellectually equivalent to children, were now deemed cognitively suited to oversee many different tasks at once. In her book *The Second Shift* (1989), the American sociologist Arlie Russell Hochschild illustrates how this new juggler should act: 'she has managed to combine what 150 years of industrialization have split wide apart – child and job, frill and suit, female culture and male.'[30]

I'd like to take a small detour and dwell a little on the flip side of the multitasking woman.

In Western culture, a familiar gender dynamic portrays men as idiots and women as socially intelligent and competent, from Homer and Marge Simpson to *The King of Queens* to Peppa Pig's parents. For men like Boris Johnson and Donald Trump, their obvious incompetence does not disqualify them from power but is rather

deficit < 186

The first cover of *Ms. Magazine* from 1972 wrestled with the woman as multitasker.

interpreted as a sign of some grand insight into the inner mechanics of the world that the rest of us don't have. Meanwhile, the pragmatic, multifaceted problem solving that is primarily represented by the multitasking women who work for these men is dismissed. You might recognise the secretary archetype: she works, but she's also a mother, and still, she must take social and emotional responsibility for the workplace to a much greater extent than her male counterparts. She is competent and flexible – but no genius.

A 2022 study of gender in the natural sciences in Danish universities included this statement from a teacher:

> The straight-A girls, we all have them in our courses and as a teacher it's delightful to have them because they show up, they've read their stuff ... They become tremendously capable – no doubt about it – but it's just, they are not the ones you, like, notice. They aren't extroverted, necessarily. But then, statistically speaking, there are a few boys. They ask questions the first day where you don't know the answer and as a teacher you just go 'Pff, what's happening here?!' And those are to ones who end up becoming, you know, hunters ...[31]

The simultaneous cleverness and stupidity of men in Western culture has been explained in many ways. Sociologists use terms like *weaponised incompetence* (intentionally pretending to be inept to get out of doing certain tasks) to explain why women in heterosexual relationships often feel their partner can figure out complicated pension schemes but not whether their child should wear a hat or not.[32] Or why a man who can make a 200-million-dollar deal can't figure out what to buy for the family breakfast.

For men who have used this strategy consciously or semi-consciously, it probably helps that they have grown up with a steady stream of culture that portrays men as ignorant but loveable fools. But even though there might be traction in this framing of men as intentionally incompetent in the area of care, I think that this image does everyone a disservice because it contributes to the underestimation of the enormous difficulty of providing care, especially when children are involved. Which is often more difficult than much paid work.

Care requires social sensibility, comprehensive knowledge, empathy and intelligence. It requires the capacity to set one's own needs aside, and to interpret complex signals from people who don't have the language or cognitive skills to express themselves adequately. This requires a sustained patience and learning, as many repeated mistakes can have long-term consequences for the child's well-being. At the same time, this work – as opposed to waged work – takes place in a strange shadowland where there is no real connection between the amount of time you have and the amount of work that needs to be done. Sixty-five per cent of Nordic fathers claim that they live in a relationship in which caretaking tasks are equally distributed. Only 45 per cent of mothers agree.[33] And when unpaid care is invisible in economics, this means that there is no official record of the time it takes out of your day if there is a small person in your home who will die if you don't do basically everything for them. And if your child needs more than the average, then too bad for you.

No child is alike, but some children take more time than others. If you have a child with a physical or cognitive disability or chronic illness, these issues intensify. Then parenthood often entails an encounter with a deeply complex bureaucratic system. A 2019 study by the Danish organisation For Lige Vilkår found that 89 per cent of parents with disabled or chronically sick children believed they often or always 'had to perform all tasks related to the administrative processing of securing state support for their children.' An anonymous parent wrote that these tasks included 'seeking knowledge, familiarity with disability law, appealing decisions that break human rights or disability law, prosthetics, doctor's statements, lost earnings, reminding them to do their job and repeatedly sending reminders for everything including lost earnings over many months.' Another wrote quite simply: 'I coordinate everything.'[34] Across Europe, 16 per cent of women say that they are entirely responsible for the household and not in paid work due to care work. In families with disabled children, the number is 26 per cent. We have built a job market with a very narrow definition of 'normal' adults. But we have also built a childcare, education system and public sphere with a very narrow understanding of the 'normal' child. When funding for taking care of disabled people is cut, women often act as 'buffers' and take over that work instead.[35] As a result, families with disabled children throughout the world have a harder time meeting their financial needs compared to families without disabled children.

I must stress, here, that there is no scientific evidence that women are better multitaskers than men. The figure of the multitasker just culturally diminishes the complexity of care and is difficult to resist because it is packaged as a kind of compliment. A research project on cognitive capabilities across gender from 2019 was published with the apt title: 'Women aren't better at multitasking than men – they just do more.'[36]

TWO TRAGEDIES

Gender roles are often the consequence of cultural disciplining with a hidden economic goal. The nuclear family ideally needs to include a person who will prioritise the market: they will produce and create economic growth. They are praised if they succeed in this, are respected with a pat on the back and money. If they don't manage to provide for their families, they are degraded and humiliated. This role has historically belonged to men.

The nuclear family also requires one of its members to freely and cheaply reproduce the workforce at home and often at their jobs as well, without having proper time or resources for this work. Culture tells them that this is the only thing that gives their life meaning, and that they should be happy and grateful for the joys of caregiving. If they are unhappy or unwilling to perform this work, they are branded as aberrant, frightening and selfish. Women typically play this role. No matter which genders are represented in a set of parents, these two roles are basically the only options. This is culture, but it is also economics.

As a result, we are left with two indescribable tragedies: a group of people, usually men, who are denied care and closeness to the home. And a group of people, usually women, are economically punished and limited in their actualisation outside the home. Both spheres have pros and cons, strengths and weaknesses – and both spheres create value.

But only the domestic sphere is seen as valueless, and both tragedies are rooted in this fact. This is one of multiple reasons why, in 2023, earmarked paternity leave in Denmark (in my opinion, an essential tool for giving men and children the right to care for each other) had to be distributed at the cost of women's existing leave. A similar thing has happened in the UK, where shared parental leave was also instituted so that a father's leave cuts into the mother's. In America, there is hardly any leave at all. The quicker the parent is out of the home, the cheaper it seems in the grand GDP picture; what is created in the home is seen as an expense, not an investment in children or their parents. The birth of a child needs to have as little impact as possible on the work lives of its parents. To stay economically valuable while also raising children, screens have conveniently become the most economically optimal form of childcare in the calculations of the state and often to families. With screens, not one adult needs to waste a single minute on something that can't be measured – namely, time spent looking a child in the eyes. If you're lucky, children might even be looking at advertising, increasing product demand! The prevalence of screens in families is the result of an economic structure in which time spent with children needs to be kept to the absolute minimum. Screen-rearing is a source of great shame to many parents, but they should know that it is a feature, not a bug. What could be more optimal than a child, alone, while their parents create value on their own screen? In 2017, Netflix named their most feared competitor: sleep.[37] There's not an unpriced minute in sight.

When freedom is defined as freedom from receiving or giving care, this always means that there will be an invisible, devalued person (or screen!), performing that work instead. They might be doing this because of their gender, race, ethnicity, finances or a combination of all of these things. Care can be done for pay or for free. It can be performed with joy or sorrow. But not everyone is 'free' to create the monetary value that men (more often) do now. This value relies on the existence of cheap care. From cradle to grave.

A society in which women's lives are identical to men's would make families impossible, at least as we know them today. However, a society in which men's lives resembled women's would give families more time to spend together, and men a break from work. Which model creates the most value? There is no neutral, quantifiable answer. Ultimately, the answer depends on whether we believe that there is value in maintaining what we have and those we love.

The Australian nurse Bronnie Ware recounts in her book *The Top Five Regrets of the Dying* how she always asked people on their deathbeds whether they regretted anything. Every single man said that they had worked too much.[38]

ISOLATED OPTIMISATION

'An hour, once it lodges in the queer element of the human spirit, may be stretched to fifty or a hundred times its clock length; on the other hand, an hour may be accurately represented by the timepiece of the mind by one second.'

VIRGINIA WOOLF, ORLANDO

CHAPTER 7

In 1899, the American neoclassical economist John Bates Clark wrote in his book *The Distribution of Wealth* that: 'the distribution of the income of society is controlled by a natural law, and this law, if it worked without friction, would give to every agent of production the amount of wealth which that agent creates.' With that, Clark assumed, whether consciously or not, an ideological standpoint disguised as an economic one: that human contributions to the economy corresponded to their income.[1] This view has cast a long shadow over our culture, even after many economists have shown that there isn't much truth to it.

The Western world is experiencing a mental health crisis. Economists are scratching their heads trying to figure it out. They struggle to understand why people are feeling like shit and continuing to say in surveys that they are doing 'poorly', because this doesn't match the numbers. We are very rich, many of us are getting richer, and many of us have jobs.

The phenomenon has been called a *Vibecession* because it is characterised by bad vibes rather than bad economic indicators.[2] In the United States and the UK, there is talk of a friendship recession. In 2023, the WHO declared that the world was experiencing a loneliness epidemic.[3] In the 15 original EU member states, GDP per capita has risen by 32 per cent between 1995 and 2018, but the experience of a good life has only risen 10 per cent.[4] In 2010, 10 per cent of Danes claimed to be struggling mentally. In 2021, that number was 17.4 per cent.[5] According to the World Economic Forum, the happiness of young people all over the globe is sinking.[6] Bad vibes all around. Even with increasing inequality and rising costs of housing, many people have jobs, a place to live and money in their bank account, but there is an incredible human deficit, and it's getting worse. In chapter 5, when we looked at GDP, we saw part of the answer: we don't measure the things that are difficult to quantify – which we then lose. But another part of the answer, I think, lies in how the language of economics has infiltrated our workplaces and shaped how we understand our own worth.

HARDER, BETTER, FASTER, STRONGER

In her book *Undoing the Demos*, the philosopher Wendy Brown argues that the primary mark of established economics in culture is that everyone sees themselves as if they were a company on the market, and our perpetual task is to develop our personal brands.[7] The state and other communities should ideally interfere as little as possible in people's individual, economic competition with one another. In politics and public debate, if one does hear arguments for care it is called an 'investment' in oneself and one's future earnings and value: you see a therapist to be able to work efficiently, you exercise to increase your dating market value, socialise to have a good 'network', read to optimise your knowledge. We have become as afraid of being worthless and unproductive as companies are.

Everything from dating to friendships is seen as a 'market' where some people have high value and others low value, no matter their gender. There should ideally be high 'demand' for you as a person. And just like in business, a person who isn't successful is like a poorly run company: weak, not worth investing in.

The economic anthropologist Karl Polanyi argued all the way back in 1944 that we were moving in the direction of a 'market society', in which all human relationships are based on monetary relationships instead of community and reciprocity.[8]

In established economics, this approach to the individual is called human capital theory. Each human is seen as a company that can be invested in, and each person has an amount of capital: education, health, social relationships. We need to keep improving, become more effective, peel back everything that doesn't serve some concrete, optimising function. Economic theories have become our self-image. At work we are products, first and foremost. What has it meant for us that the dominant discipline in our society only sees what can be quantified?

MUSHROOM AT WORK

In 2017, I went to a party at my good friend Mia's office, an architecture firm. She had worked there for a long time, and I had the impression she enjoyed it. We were having a beer with two of her colleagues and talking about the company when one of them said: 'But now the party's over. We've been bought out.' He explained that a private equity firm had swallowed the company. Even though the bosses had said that the takeover wouldn't affect daily operations, Mia's colleague was less optimistic: 'The same thing happened at my friend's work,' he explained. 'And it made his life a living hell.'

A few months later, Mia and I were getting dinner with a few of our friends. I asked how the acquisition was going. 'Terrible ... everything I liked about my job: gone. There isn't the same freedom there used to be. All I do now is enter my hours,' she said. Another friend who worked at a large communications firm interjected: 'Timekeeping! Ugh! Kill me now! The absolute worst!' They explained that they now spent the majority of their time registering exactly how they spent their time. Which clients, which projects, which programmes, in what networks – and what were the measurable results? She had previously focused on delivering great work to the client, but it now seemed like she was working for a bunch of strangers in the private equity firm. 'They have to know exactly what I'm doing every single second. And then they had the nerve to get rid of the free beer on Fridays.'

My friend was lucky that day. I spared her a lecture (can you imagine being friends with me? Nightmare.) but established economic thinking had dug its claws into her company, or at least an offshoot of it called Taylorism.

In the 1910s, Frederick Winslow Taylor took the mechanisation of economics to the next level and set out to structure the workplace so that it would function like a well-oiled machine.[9] He called this *scientific management* (you might notice, again, how anything that involves numbers gets called scientific, and everything that doesn't becomes unscientific).[10]

Taylor's focus was the automotive factory. Here, there were both specialised and unspecialised workers, and the specialised workers had a lot of responsibility. They knew, for example, how to weld the main parts of a car. They were difficult to fire or push around. The welders knew that it would be difficult to replace them, so they tended to demand better working conditions and pay raises. To Taylor, this made the process less efficient, and maybe more expensive. He suggested instead that everyone should be given a clear, simple task. Once the tasks were defined, a person could be 'plugged into' each one. This made employees more interchangeable, in case they acted out. Instead of having one extremely skilled welder, companies would hire three unskilled workers who were trained to execute a small part of the welder's job again and again and again. Thus you could fire the skilled welder and divide his salary between the three unskilled workers. Taylor wrote: 'It is only through *enforced* standardization of methods ... that this faster work can be assured ... The *management* must supply continually one or more teachers to show each new man the new and simpler motions, and the slower men must be constantly watched and helped until they have risen to their proper speed ... All of this involves an individual study of and treatment for each man, while in the past they have been handled in large groups.'[11] Some of you might recognise this centralized enforcement from your own place of work. You are not a team doing something together, you are individuals competing against each other, all replaceable. Bad vibes indeed.

The private equity firm had performed a similar analysis of my friend Mia's workplace. And there, Mia had stuck out like a worrisome skilled welder. Not because she complained, but because her role was porous and social. Previously Mia would move around the office, chiming in here and there on different projects and exchanging ideas with colleagues from other departments at the Friday happy hour, but this made it difficult to measure exactly how much value Mia was creating for the company relative to other employees. This meant that she was the most dangerous thing a worker can be in the modern workplace: unmeasurable, and therefore irreplaceable. If she asked for a raise or decided to switch jobs, the private equity company would have difficulty finding a new Mia because they wouldn't know exactly where her skills were at play. She therefore had to be monitored and mechanised. They had to know exactly what she was doing, so that if a new Mia was needed, the transition wouldn't be too troublesome. Of course, this made Mia easier to fire and robbed her of her autonomy – and her enjoyment of her work.

Many have called this development a bureaucratisation of work life. But the point is actually the same one that runs all the way through economic cultural history: Mia needed to become a cog in the machine.

The strategy aimed to 'isolate' Mia, so that the private equity firm could determine exactly how much 'value' she created per hour. Then they could assess whether they were getting enough *benefit* out of Mia compared to her *cost*.

The American Federation of Labor was already critical of Taylorism's 'scientific' approach to work in the 1920s. They wrote that it 'looks upon the worker as a mere instrument of production and reduces him to a semi-automatic attachment to the machine or tool.'[12] The view of the human as an extension of a mechanical process has created a complicated relationship between the employer and the employee.

Funnily enough, it was in the 1980s, when scientific management entered the office after having conquered the factory, that bosses started referring to their employees as 'family'. When people felt dehumanised, they had to be instilled with the sense that they were obligated to care about their work and colleagues – maybe because their jobs clearly did not care about them. This belief that workers have to provide the social glue has become one of the defining features of the modern workplace.

In our day, the rise of AI and more nuanced surveillance technologies has intensified the focus on individual productivity. The tech magazine *Wired* has called software that is used to surveil employees 'bossware'.[13] Five thousand workplaces in 12 countries use a software called Teramind to keep an eye on their employees' emails, messages, phone conversations and internet history, as well as which files they open at which times. A report on the practice suggests that 70 per cent of all large employers will use some form of surveillance technology in 2025.[14]

Back to Mia's terrible job. In the book *Our Lives in Their Portfolios* (2023), professor of political economy Brett Christophers explains how private equity acquisitions are becoming increasingly commonplace.[15] A private equity firm is an investment firm that invests in companies or property. Their money usually comes from pension funds, private trusts or very wealthy individuals. The task of the private equity firm is to get

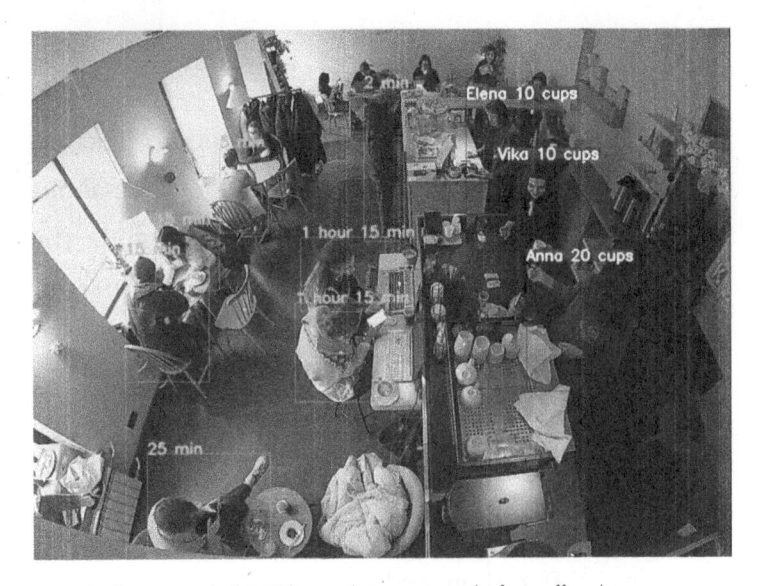

In the autumn of 2023, a video went viral of a coffeeshop where new AI technology was using facial recognition software to measure how many cups of coffee each barista had made, how often they washed their hands, where they went, and how long customers spent at their tables. Source: YouTube / Neurospot

the highest possible return on investment when they sell the company again. This means that the private equity firm typically doesn't care much about Mia or her colleagues, or about whether or not they've had a 'good day'. This is not their concern. Instead, they use complex methods to measure value creation in the company to figure out what and who is creating the most value for the bottom line and then they strip back everything else. They need to make a profit, no matter what invisible deficits they create for their employees. Private equity firms usually hang on to their investments for three to seven years. A lot can happen in that time when attention is only paid to the value creation that can be measured by numbers.

In their book *The Big Con*, the economist Mariana Mazzucato and the political economist Rosie Collington write that viewing employees as individual human capital can have serious implications for the entire way that we think about innovation and training. And this is one of the main reasons that so many organisations have become dependent on buying knowledge from management consultants – because they assume 'that capabilities can be conjured up at will, and that knowledge can simply be purchased, as though off the shelf. It assumes learning in the contracting organisation is not an incremental and collective *process* but a *transaction*.'[16] Since consultants are unable to capture the value of social interactions, they believe that you can buy the effects that social processes usually create, as if they were products.

This is completely inconsistent with what research tells us: that learning happens in social interactions among employees and is a consequence of who they are as people, not just as bundles of capital. Collington and Mazzucato write that learning is often: 'a know-how built up over time, which is harder to quantify or capture completely.'[17] Here we encounter the same problem that GDP had with estimating unpaid work. If you use economic metrics, the consequence will be that everything that creates collective, emotional and social value will disappear.

Mazzucato and Collington argue that this form of effectivisation results in the 'infantilisation' of institutions in both the private and public sectors. It is simply impossible to become a mature, adult organisation with experience when everyone is supposed to be replaceable. External consultants are hired to plan cutbacks and restructurings entirely unaware of the social dynamics and human experiences that are not reflected on the employees' CVs. As a result, consultants hollow out what Mazzucato and Collington call the organisation's collective memory.[18]

In 2006, a group of consultants concluded that 40 per cent of employees in the Danish tax collections authority could be fired without any loss in the quality of the work. Many of the people fired were older, as the new 'scientific' measure of success was 'customer satisfaction'. Fifteen years later, the consequences were clear: we were looking at a social breakdown. The Danish public had been swindled out of 12.6 billion kroner. A group of sociologists described the collapse like this: 'The employees lost their social anchor as they found it hard to communicate. The deteriorating social relations combined with the fact that people simply did not know one another, had dire effects on the collapse of meaning.'[19] When employees aren't seen as people, and workplaces aren't seen as collectives, the importance of social interaction in creating value, solving problems, getting ideas and building dignified, enjoyable work disappears. A workplace with no care is a workplace that cannot perform basic tasks.

PUNISHED FOR CARING

As a consequence of these metrics, employees who have the audacity to spend time on collective projects and social undertakings see their careers curtailed.

In the book *The No Club*, the economist Lise Vesterlund, along with several others, calls these immeasurable chores non-promotable tasks.[20] In an interview with the Danish media outlet *Zetland*, Vesterlund puts it this way: 'Non-promotable tasks help the organisation but not the person doing the work. Everyone does non-promotable tasks and the kind one does is defined by your role in the workplace, and your rank ... But the most common kind in for-profit organisations is work that doesn't create a profit. This might be training new employees. Or colleagues asking you to help them. Reading through other employees' presentations, or having clients that might not pay a lot, but who are very time-consuming.'[21] In other words, the work that makes all other work possible, but which can't be measured by economic metrics for the bottom line, is not seen as 'creating a profit'. But this is also work that created joy for a person like Mia. She didn't enjoy working as if she were completely isolated from her colleagues and only thinking about her role in the company's bottom line.

In 2019, a debate was sparked in Denmark when a female consultant wrote that if you wanted to get ahead in your career, you shouldn't bake for your colleagues because it wouldn't be counted as part of the bottom line.[22] *The No Club* offers ample evidence of women's over-representation in non-promotable tasks in the United States. However, these results also show that abandoning this work is easier said than done: 'Women were not rewarded when they helped, but when they didn't, they were penalized ... when men didn't help they weren't penalized, and when they helped, they were rewarded.'[23] So you can't just stop baking cupcakes overnight. The researchers estimated that at the big firms they had studied, women did about 200 hours more of this type of work every year than men.

The economic care paradox is summed up nicely here. The caring woman isn't respected for her knowledge and skills because care doesn't make a profit, but she is 100 per cent expected to perform the care anyway, and if she doesn't, she's a bitch. Some people *must* take care of the social work among employees, but as long as its value is invisible, either that work is done at great cost to the employee doing it or you have a workplace where no one takes any social responsibility. Private equity firms? They sell the company for a profit, the bottom line swells and GDP grows, while the social deficits these methods create aren't registered anywhere. As Bruce Flatt, CEO of the gigantic global investment firm Brookfield, told the *Financial Times* in 2018: 'what we do is behind the scenes. Nobody knows we're there.'[24]

And Mia? Now all our nights out start with: 'My job puts me in such a bad mood.'

MULTIFACETED MACHINES

Measurability and organisational streamlining can also determine what kinds of people there are room for. A well-oiled watch can't accommodate a square gear. When each employee is evaluated as an individual, this can skew the perception of their contributions because what they give or take from the community is not represented – so we don't see, for example, if they have been discriminated against by their colleagues. This is worth noting in current conversations about diversity and inclusion in the workplace. Because while we are experiencing a kind of cultural break from the terrible ways that people have been kept from fair and dignified working conditions, our economic management tools are pulling in the opposite direction.

One statistic I haven't been able to get out of my mind says that employment among vision-impaired people in Denmark was twice as high in 1975 as it is today. Back then, 20 per cent of vision-impaired people of working age had a paid job. Today the number is only 10 per cent.[25]

Poul Lüneborg, the former president of Blindehistorisk Selskab (Society for the History of the Blind), says of the change: 'In a competitive labour market, where many are afraid of not being able to handle daily challenges, there is less tolerance. Increased efficiency leads to less tolerance.'[26] Lüneborg uses the word efficiency in a throwaway manner here, but what he means is of course quantifiable efficiency. Each person needs to create value, be measurable and fit into a 'place'. There are many tasks that someone with a visual impairment can do, but this requires a space in which care is taken to adapt the workflow to this person.

In December 2023, a 'heartwarming' story spread through Denmark. The broadcast network TV2 covered a young man with infantile autism who was working in a hardware supply warehouse and doing great. All of his colleagues loved him. He had held the job for two and a half years and the company was no longer receiving a subsidy from the foundation that had helped him get the job in the first place. The company, in other words, hadn't paid the cost of his onboarding.[27] This man is an effective worker today, but his neurodivergence means that the hardware supply store wouldn't have invested in him without government aid. He had to be optimal in all capacities, and this means that even small human variations can be perceived as massive economic burdens. In a cost-benefit analysis, the definition of normal is very narrow. An American study from 2006 showed that a large part of why people with disabilities were not hired was a *perception* that there would be a negative cost-benefit. But looking at the 'indirect benefits', it turned out that the long-term positive effects of a more accessible workplace would create value for many employees.[28,29]

Forty-nine thousand people with disabilities in Denmark are unemployed, even though they would like to work.[30] In so-called developing countries, estimates point to upward of 80–90 per cent of people with disabilities being unemployed. In industrialised countries the number is estimated to be around 50–70 per cent.[31]

We have created workplaces and societies in which you are rewarded for acting in your own best interest, and then when people act that way, it is claimed to be an expression of human nature, but *The No Club*'s studies show that people tend to be penalised at work for taking on the kind of social responsibility that diversity requires. When care is not seen as an effective or valuable way to spend work hours, fewer and fewer people will do it, even though they might like to.

Similar dynamics are worth considering in terms of linguistic and cultural diversity. A large-scale study of racism in the European labour market from 2017 showed that racialised Europeans and migrants were less likely to be invited to interviews, were overrepresented in tougher jobs with lower pay, and that experiences of discrimination in the workplace were commonplace across the continent.[32]

If a person has difficulty fitting into the culture, they can appear less 'effective' in economic assessments of their productivity. When everything comes down to a simple bottom line based on distinct individuals, then frictionless exchange between workers is preferred. If you are discriminated against or excluded from social or work-related spaces, of course you are going to seem less effective. The bounds of normality shrink. The optimal person is the person who has the lowest cost and the highest benefit. If it takes time for an employee to be socially accepted, they will seem 'expensive'.

Part of what makes us cheaper is being more similar. When we try to encourage cultural diversity in an economically streamlined environment, this creates all kinds of paradoxes for the employees from minority backgrounds. As Mustafa F. Özbilgin, professor of organisation theory at Brunel University in London, and Natalia Slutskaya, professor of work and organisational studies at the University of Sussex write, this can mean that 'minority status' becomes yet another component of human capital, because you contribute 'diversity' which is now seen as a plus in many contexts. But you're still supposed to compete with those who belong to the majority group and be a good 'business case'.[33] If you don't succeed in that, it is seen as your own fault rather than a problem with the social structure. In other words, you have to sell your 'diversity' as a product, even though that 'diversity' might be the thing that prevents you from being seen as a good deal.

The centralisation of decision-making, as experienced by my friend Mia, and the work of external consultants, can also mean the disappearance of local, social considerations. When decisions about who is most valuable are made far away from a company's employees, it is difficult to be compassionate about the very simple fact that people are different, get sick, have kids, burn out, get divorced and so on. There is often distance between those who are structuring and evaluating the employees and those managing them in practice.

Maybe this is why everyone hates middle management (sorry, middle managers, but ...). Middle managers are responsible for dealing with real people, using decisions that are often made using established economic methods. Middle managers see their subordinates every single day and are aware of their internal differences, life situations and skills. They are also familiar with their personalities and might see opportunities for collaboration that people further up the ladder might not see. They know us, and we feel betrayed all the more when they treat us like numbers. Research from the Danish Finance Federation showed that employees who were evaluated on an individual basis were twice as likely to be stressed as those who were evaluated collectively.[34]

In Denmark, we often talk about the 46,000 young people who do not have jobs or education.[35] But we rarely mention that 40 per cent of these people have a disability.

When we work with very simple understandings of value, we end up with very simple understandings of who has value and who there is space for. A cost-benefit analysis creates a conception of the 'normal' employee that is very difficult to measure up to. We can organise as many diversity seminars as we want, but if there are neither adequate resources for care nor any collective understanding of value, there will never be diversity.

A SHORT FUTURE

These economic tools have also made their way into the NGO world, where I used to work. Both organisations and foundations, understandably, want to be able to measure the impact of the work they do. Foundations want to be able to show their donors a graph that documents the direct correlation between their donation and some exact number of people whose lives have been measurably improved as a consequence. But this can mean that investments are made in areas that are easy to measure instead of ones that make a difference in people's lives.

The former administrator of the United States Agency for International Development (USAID), Andrew Natsios, has said that 'those development programs that are most precisely and easily measured are the least transformational, and those programs that are the most transformational are the least measurable.'[36] Possibly this is because the most transformative political initiatives involve complex social relationships that have enormously different impacts on different people and create long-term value that is difficult to predict. A cost-benefit analysis might seem like a simple, neutral method of assessment, but it can mean that people put their energy into reaching key performance indicators instead of making an impact. This is called Goodhart's law: 'When a measure becomes a target, it ceases to be a good measure.'

This is true of art, leisure, sports, theatre, community engagement – the list goes on and on. We live in a time where everyone needs to measure what they produce and how effective they are. So we search and search for a way to quantify what we do and why it is good. Who hasn't been in a meeting where someone excitedly shares that a Facebook post has got 40,000 engagements, while everyone around the table, staring blankly, is thinking to themselves: what the hell does that mean? Having more data doesn't necessarily make us smarter. It can also make us dumber.[37]

Care moves between people and it is rarely captured by a salary or measures of individual human capital. This is true of all kinds of care, including those that aren't directly related to reproduction. When only quantifiable results matter, it has a chilling effect on us all. At work we withhold care even though we might want to give it, fearing that we will be punished. We sense that even the smallest difference or the smallest inefficiency will deprive us of essential value and be met with judgement. We are well aware that we are being measured and weighed all the time. Big money, bad vibes.

A DISSERVICE TO PUBLIC SERVICES

'The "well" person is the person well enough to go to work. The "sick" person is the one who can't ... When sickness is temporary, care is not normal.'

JOHANNA HEDVA, *SICK WOMAN THEORY*

In 2019, I was admitted to Bispebjerg Hospital in Copenhagen. As I've previously mentioned, I suffer from a chronic illness called ulcerative colitis, and it was flaring up. I was very happy to be admitted to Bispebjerg. Martin Nyrop, the architect who designed the hospital, was an advocate for what was called 'healing architecture'. As a result, Bispebjerg, built in 1913, is bright and airy, with large windows, art on the walls and beautiful gardens that patients can walk around in. Light and air would have a hard time in a cost-benefit analysis today. Windows are expensive. For some people, it wouldn't make a difference. But for me, it did.

This was the first time in my life I had been admitted to hospital, and I spent five days and five nights there. It was an opportunity to see how care is organised when people are paid to do it. Anyone who has spent time in a hospital knows that you might see a doctor for a total of five minutes a day. The rest of the time, nurses and care workers are the ones making

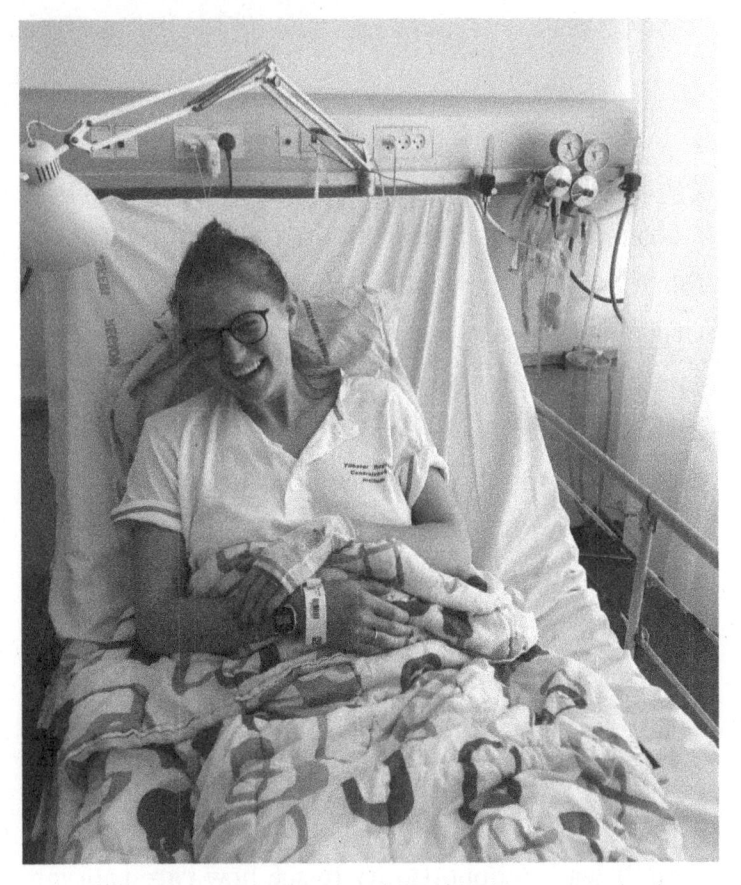

Bispebjerg Hospital, 2019. Photo by my friend Steve McFarland.

things happen. I was completely overwhelmed by the sheer variety of tasks they oversaw. There was an older woman who was lonely and wanted someone to talk to. There were blood tests. There were medical records to be updated. There was food. Thousands of different combinations of medicines. There were drainage tubes, blood pressures, migraines, a patient with dementia; someone who needed to be prepped for surgery; someone who needed a shower or to use the bathroom.

I wouldn't be writing this book without the efforts of the staff there. I haven't been admitted to the hospital since, but I am in touch with the paid, public care system at least once every three months, when I have blood drawn to make sure that the immunosuppressants are doing what they're supposed to. A lot of work is necessary to maintain me. I actually have pretty bad scoliosis too. A hundred years ago – before we had public healthcare – I would probably be dead.

When it comes to my illness, physical and mental health are closely linked. Flare-ups usually happen in times of stress or change. I need stability if I'm supposed to be healthy. I can't afford to split my mind from my body, as Western philosophy has tried to make us do for the past 400 years.

Lying in my hospital bed, I wondered how the political system calculated the value created by a nurse.

It took months for me to understand that according to state accounting, all the care I had received was money wasted.

RETURN OF THE ROBOT

The dominant approach in today's macroeconomics is the DSGE model, which is also known as an equilibrium model (DSGE = dynamic stochastic general equilibrium).[1] The economist Servaas Storm has called these models 'straightjackets' that economists have to work with to be accepted by the macroeconomic community.[2] DSGE models are used to evaluate politics, make prognoses about the future and simulate real economies in academic research. They exist in national economic institutions all over the world. Italy has IGEMs, England has COMPASS, Denmark has MAKRO, the International Monetary Fund (IMF) has GIMF, Chile has XMAS, Brazil has SAMBA (props to them for at least coming up with a fun name!) and so on and so on. DSGE models shape politics at all levels across the globe.

All economic models tell a story about society and its inhabitants, whether or not they intend to. They create worlds. This is how our world looks in a standard DSGE model:

- People live forever.[3]
- People are utility maximisers with perfect foresight (in other words, clairvoyant robots). And everyone is *the same*.
- Individuals are not affected by communities such as families and they are at no point 'born'. (The mushroom plot thickens!)
- Unemployment is always voluntary, because there is always low paid work available. All activity that isn't paid is 'leisure'.
- No one is disabled or gets sick. Actually, no one has a body.
- Markets are always in equilibrium and work seamlessly, as long as they are not disturbed by state intervention or shocks, such as war or major technological change. Equilibrium is a mechanical process that ensures everyone receives the pay they deserve and the goods they need at a price that reflects their value (*If it still sounds too good to be true, it probably still is*).

This chapter is the story of these models and their role in your life.

In the 1970s, the Western world experienced economic crises never observed before. This opened the door for a new paradigm in macroeconomics, which is the part of the discipline that considers all of society. After a period of broad economic agreement about the necessity of the welfare state and scepticism about the supremacy of the market with Keynes at the intellectual helm, another world view emerged. Economists dived deeper into theory and moved further away from reality. And this changed the entire language of power.

An economist called Robert Lucas was especially central to the new macroeconomic culture shift.[4] He didn't believe that Keynesian macroeconomic models held water anymore. Along with other economists (many of them up-and-coming), he criticised the earlier models for being based on historical observations instead of natural laws and mathematics.[5] In order to bolster macroeconomics and make it more rigorous, Lucas believed it needed to rest on so-called micro-foundations. Just as everything in the world is made up of atoms, he felt that a good model of society should be built on micro-foundations. Without reliable laws governing human behaviour, it would not be possible to predict the future or offer political advice. The desire for a mechanical world, by this time so deep-rooted in our psyche, was the driving force of this project. Economists in the 1980s therefore built a macroeconomic model based on what they called the representative agent.⁶ Marginalism's fake hypothetical person, which had been buried in the Keynesian period, was back from the dead!

As macroeconomics became more mathematical, it started to play a larger role in advising politicians. The sociologists Elizabeth Popp Berman and Daniel Hirschman have shown that economists in the 1970s and 80s achieved what they called professional authority.⁷ I believe that this is also what economists have in our culture today. Economics is seen as the only neutral social science, and statements made by economists are often taken as unassailable truths. As Lucas himself summed up in 2004: 'Economic theory is mathematical analysis. Everything else is just pictures and talk.'⁸

Using the representative agent (aka the clairvoyant robot), politicians and social servants alike believed that economic tools like cost-benefit analysis could be used to determine whether certain policies were good or bad. Popp Berman has observed that people working for the government and politicians started to adopt an *economic style of thinking*. She describes this mode of thought: 'Its implicit theory of politics imagined that disinterested technocrats could make reasonably neutral, apolitical decisions. The economic style tended to downplay competing concerns about rights, equality, power, democratic process, and the politics of making policy, subordinating them to efficiency in ways that seems justifiable from the economic perspective, but often seemed misguided to others.'[9] Efficiency became the new political target, and in true economic style, it is most efficient to see people as self-interested robots motivated by money. Competition thus becomes the smartest way to achieve goals. People won't do anything good or beautiful if left to their own devices, so we build policy based on that assumption.

The more technical and mechanical the economic conversation became, the more it seemed like scientific, apolitical economic advice. It is difficult to see an opinion when it is hidden behind 25 equations and a model. But as we'll see, this doesn't mean that opinions aren't there.

Katherine Moos, an economist who has specialised in the welfare state, has argued that after Robert Lucas' demands for micro-foundations in the 1980s, macroeconomic models took on a 'nihilistic' view of the role of the state in the economy. Because the market was mechanical and effective, while politics was human and fallible, politics started to be feared in economic and political circles. People lost faith in the belief that politics could improve our lives. Moos writes: 'Focusing on policy evaluation, the Lucas critique renders the traditional view of policy as without meaning or value ... If econometric models cannot produce accurate forecasts or predictions, then this implies that a meaningful policy is impossible or far-fetched.'[10] She concludes that economic policy started to focus mainly on keeping the market stable and protecting it from unpredictable chaos, such as large public investments. So much for solving problems like poverty, inequality or education, or anything else that didn't lend itself to ostensibly perfect prediction.[11]

The nihilism that Moos refers to perfectly sums up Lucas' own personal position. In 1982, he was asked whether social injustice existed. His answer was yes, because 'governments involve social injustice' by intervening in the market.[12]

This type of anti-state nihilism is clear in the equilibrium models that shape almost all economic policy today. Back in the 1980s, Lars Andersen from the Danish Economic Council of the Labour Movement wrote that if this new type of economic model were implemented to assess policy in Denmark, 'we need to be aware that this will be the same as declaring that public services have no value.'[13] And so it was. After the introduction of general equilibrium models in Denmark, it didn't matter whether public money was spent hosting the Grand Départ in the Tour de France or giving a prematurely born child oxygen. In these models, taxes had the same (negative) consequence, namely that they skewed market equilibrium.[14]

The person these models are based on, who doesn't have a mind or a body and lives forever, naturally doesn't need to be kept healthy, happy or alive. The models assume that people exist on their own, completely independently of others. Four hundred years after Hobbes' fungi, here we are.

The triumph of these equilibrium models has been hard on people working with services that are difficult to measure, and even harder on those who need these services to survive. (Economists were pretty embarrassed in the 2000s when it became more publicly known that the representative agent in the models was immortal. But nothing material was changed – now the representative agent is just called a dynastic household. The household still behaves like one person and exists in eternity.)

WHEN YOU KNOW THE 'COST' BUT NOT THE 'BENEFIT'

Sometimes people will joke that economists know the price of everything and value of nothing. That somewhat snide joke is a caricature, but when it comes to care in the DSGE models, it is actually true: in them, price is the only measure of value.

The prevalence of equilibrium models in major institutions like the World Bank, the International Monetary Fund (IMF) and nations across the world has meant that care in the public sector has exclusively been seen as a state expenditure. These models do not figure in any positive effects, and therefore, officially, care doesn't create value; it takes it. The costs of care are made clear, sparking plenty of lively debates about how care is an expense, a burden, something that needs to be cut to keep our economies afloat. But we have no equivalent clarity – and certainly no number – when it comes to describing the benefits of care. We can't calculate what it would mean for society if it *wasn't there*.

According to the DSGE models, we might as well set a nurse's salary on fire, as the economic effect would be the same. In some countries, economists have made conservative and small estimates that education might improve productivity somewhat, but that is it. Money spent on care appears to be an unnecessary expense that might even be detrimental to the market. Economists often say that the effects of public consumption are 'subject to considerable uncertainty'. A translation of this is: there is value somewhere in there, of course we know that, but we do not have any precise numbers, and numbers are all that matters.

This has naturally caused some raised eyebrows, particularly among people who work with care on a daily basis. In 2022, when a team of Danish economic advisers had to defend DSGE models, they maintained that there was nothing political about the exclusion of the effects of public care work. It was simply because there was not sufficient 'available evidence', and because it was 'extraordinarily difficult'.[15]

But they haven't let these shortcomings get in their way. After seven years of work, Denmark started implementing a new DSGE model in 2022, MAKRO (boring name!). In an analysis of its glorious new abilities, one economist wrote that critics shouldn't get their hopes up for something new when it came to the impact of public services like care, because the model stayed 'completely clear' of this subject.[16] Care and climate impacts, both absent in the model, were instead handled by more diminutive 'working groups'.

The models and the people that make them have taken an approach to 'evidence' that means it is 'extraordinarily difficult' to calculate the effects of the Bispebjerg gastroenterology unit, but extraordinarily easy to assume that everyone lives forever. My gut exists in reality. Immortality doesn't.

The consequences of the shortcomings of DSGE models have been immense for reproduction and care. The feminist economist Drucilla Barker has written that they force economists like her 'to conform to a paradigm that is decidedly unfit for our purposes. It cannot meaningfully address the issues we care about, especially the crises of care and social reproduction, the burdens of which fall disproportionately on the shoulders of women.'[17]

In 2004, Kenneth Arrow, who won the Nobel Prize in Economic Sciences for the theory of equilibrium in the 1970s, was asked whether marginalism's rational individual could really be used as a basis for a model of the entire economy. He responded no, and that it was 'true and unfortunate'.[18] But nevertheless these are the tools used to calculate the effects of policy every single day, all over the world, without our knowledge, and without giving us a say.

EXTRAORDINARILY DIFFICULT

So why is it 'extraordinarily difficult' for DSGE models – and perhaps macroeconomics in general – to include care work in their language? There are a few reasons.

Public care is a service whose value arises in the encounter between at least two people. Care cannot be isolated as a product. The exact value of care depends on how acutely the person being cared for needs it and their circumstances. A nurse performing a cardiac massage to save someone's life doesn't get a higher salary for those 20 minutes compared to the 10 minutes they spend fetching a patient a glass of fruit juice. Care cannot be captured by an hourly rate. A care provider completes thousands of different tasks over the course of a week, for different people with different needs and different lives.

Care is also not a 'scarce' resource in the same way that other things can be. You cannot build a car yourself if you need a car. But if care is not available on the market or from the public sector, or is not of high enough quality, someone will often step in and do it for free. This is often the case with childcare, elderly care and care for people with disabilities. For this reason, many feminist economists have observed that women act as a 'buffer' when equilibrium models encourage cuts to care budgets. Women absorb the shock and work even harder and invisibly for those they love. It is difficult to measure what the loss of paid care 'does' to the economy. But it isn't difficult to feel.

A consumer cannot evaluate the utility of care in the moment of purchase. In marginalism, the clairvoyant robot knows what the utility of a product is before it buys it. But the value of care is inscrutable. A nursery with one teacher and a nursery with five teachers both provide childcare. Five teachers are of course much more expensive than one. But you cannot do a yearly cost-benefit analysis of the utility of five extra teachers. For an under-resourced child, that difference can be a lifeline, while it might be negligible for the privileged child. (Many economists have worked to measure the value of care based on income later in life. Again, you might ask yourself whether higher income later in life is a good measure of the value created by a teacher ...)

An American study of up-front medical fees showed that patients are enormously bad at evaluating whether a doctor's visit is necessary until they have been seen.[19] Normal people don't have the professional insight that such care entails; we have no choice but to listen to the professionals. This will be familiar to anyone who has been to the dentist and been told they need to spend thousands on having a wisdom tooth pulled – speaking from experience.

Care work, fundamentally, is not just a consumer good for the individual, but for all of society. When you buy and pay for a shirt, it is yours and the money belongs to the store. This is an exchange. Society is not dramatically changed (even though resource consumption ties us to the planet!). The opposite is true of care. When I was admitted to Bispebjerg, the work done on my body enabled me to create value in all parts of society for the rest of my life. As a friend, as a lover, as a taxpayer.

In 2023, Sweden proudly announced that multiple municipalities were ending the year with a 'surplus' of money that hadn't been spent.[20] The municipalities were happy and proud. But savings on care don't necessarily mean that smart economic decisions have been made. A significant amount of value can be lost if, for example, an otherwise capable person has not received the psychological care they need. Moreover, it can destroy that person's entire family. An economic surplus can be a smokescreen that hides social deficits. Society ultimately pays the price when care doesn't work as it should.

In the established economy, it is commonly said that the private sector pays for the public sector. But value creation goes both ways. The public sector gives the private sector its most essential resource: healthy, happy and competent workers. The surplus of the public sector rests in the business world and in our joy and well-being. The cost of care tells us nothing about what it does.

All of these factors, taken together, make care very poorly suited to DSGE models because care is by definition unpredictable.[21] It has the potential to change both the carer and the person being cared for. The economic theorist William Brian Arthur has argued that the economic overreliance on mathematics has made it a science of 'nouns' – which are stable and quantifiable – and not 'verbs', which are actions and transformations: 'Because algebraic mathematics allows only quantifiable nouns and disbars verbs, it acts as a sieve. What it can't express it can't contain, so processes and actions fall through the sieve and are unexpressed. This noun-restriction causes distortions to the story economics tells.'[22]

If the most important thing about the economy is keeping it in equilibrium so that we can predict its development, then it isn't so strange that we don't invest in care. A model that assumes that its individual parts don't change over a lifetime is a model that will never embrace care. The most beautiful and essential part of care is that we have no idea where it will take us. Who could have ever foreseen what free education and free healthcare would do for an economy? Today those types of large-scale human investments seem almost impossible, having been deemed 'subject to considerable uncertainty'. Too much money spent on care is seen as a chaotic and precarious path to follow. But it is nowhere near as chaotic and precarious as a society that spends too little.

WHAT IS AN ECONOMY?

Today, calling society 'the economy' is completely mainstream in political conversation. But even though production, sales and money have always been part of politics, the concept of 'the economy' is relatively new. From 1900 until the Second World War, the word 'economy' was used twice in British political party manifestos. In both cases, it meant 'frugality'. In 2015, the word 'economy' appeared 59 times in the UK Conservative Party's manifesto in the sense that we know it today.[23] The historian Adam Tooze writes that as economists gained more influence in politics, the economy became a 'thing' that had to be monitored and controlled.[24] But this 'thing' does not currently relate to care needs in a concrete or systematic way.

The political theorist Timothy Mitchell describes this shift: 'The power of the economy as a discursive process lies exactly with fixing this effect of the real [economy] ... The proliferation of models, statistics, plans, and programs of economic discourse all claim to represent the different elements and relationships of a real object, the national-economy. Yet this object ... is itself constituted as a discursive process.'[25] In other words, nothing is objectively good for the economy because there is no objective definition of what 'the economy' means. When politicians aim to improve 'the economy', this is not a neutral position with a clear goal. We should always ask: what exactly do you mean by that? Think back to those poor Americans who, during the largest economic crisis of our time, had cleaner air in their cities because economic activity creates so much pollution. When the 'economy is doing well' and more people have jobs, they start dying again from the smoke. Something is always hiding behind the numbers. Today, a 'healthy economy' is a matter of looking very carefully at *some* numbers and ignoring others.

Diane Elson, a pioneer of feminist economics, has argued that 'Macroeconomic policies, which may be seen as "sound" in the sense of balancing the budget ... can be quite "unsound" in the sense of exacerbating real resource constraints by destroying human capabilities'.[26] Access to care and healthcare is not an integral goal of today's macroeconomic policy. Instead, media figures and politicians suggest that a 'healthy economy' will solve these problems down the line. However, exactly what role they play remains opaque and often ignored.

A SIN OF OMISSION

George Akerlof, a Nobel Prize winner in economics, has described the problem like this: 'economics as a discipline gives rewards that favour the "hard" and disfavour the "soft." Such bias leads economic research to ignore important topics and problems that are difficult to approach in a "hard" way – thereby resulting in "sins of omission."'[27] Many economists realise that this problem exists and maybe also realise that it is the 'hard' brand that gives them this 'professional authority'. But we, the public, who are served the calculations of these models, don't know it. We trust that they are capable of capturing all of society.[28]

That is why politicians and journalists are still looking for answers to 'soft' questions about care and education in macroeconomic models. It gives a sense of security, and scientificness. The answers have *enormous* weight in public discourse.

In 2023, the Danish government proposed that certain master's degree programmes should be shortened because it would be better for the Danish economy if students entered the labour force sooner. One economics commission tried to estimate the long-term effects of this. In Denmark, one of the world's richest countries with access to the world's most advanced and costly economic models, they concluded that the initiative would either cost 7 billion kroner or result in gains of 32 billion kroner.[29] The Economic Council did their own calculation, concluding that it would cost up to 14 billion.[30] A more honest answer might have been: 'We have no clue.'

These commissions and councils found it easy to calculate the cost of educating people. It was much harder to figure out what would be lost by educating them less. Now these various calculations are floating around in the public debate like accepted truths, but the fact is that no one knows what the consequences of these budget cuts will be. Charades like this are common. In 2010 the economist Edward Leamer seemed almost incredulous: 'Our understanding of causal effects in macroeconomics is virtually nil and will remain so. Don't we know that?'[31]

When you actually nose your way around the calculations of costs of policy, you will often find vehement economic disagreement.[32]

The incalculable nature of care makes it precarious and easy to cut. The historical devaluation of care throughout Western culture reaches its absolute peak at a time with almost limitless human cunning and capabilities, with a series of invisible assumptions that look something like this:

> Economics is the study of value, and so economists need to know the precise value of things
> Value is measured according to market prices because those are the only precise numbers we have
> Anything that doesn't have a price can't be measured
> Everything that can't be measured becomes an expense
> The valuelessness of care and education seems scientific and apolitical

I wouldn't be able to think, love, work and pay my taxes if I hadn't been admitted to Bispebjerg Hospital in 2019. But nowhere in the most powerful economic models is there any record of the fact that those people saved my life.

A NEUTRAL CALCULATION

After the financial crisis in 2008 and the European debt crisis in 2010, the IMF and EU decided that all countries *had* to cut public spending to signal austerity to the financial markets, balance their debts and stimulate GDP growth – that was their definition of a 'healthy economy'.

In 2022, the New Economics Foundation found that countries across Europe spent on average 1,000 euros less per capita annually on public services than they would have without the cuts following the crisis.[33] So the 'balancing' project succeeded, in a sense. The member countries reduced their debts. But the invisible consequences of this are much more difficult to measure than the visible decrease of debt. These consequences are social – they exist in our minds, bodies, homes and communities.[34]

The European Women's Lobby studied the effects of these austerity measures: women's presence on the labour market fell in 22 European countries, in part because so many women work in the public sector.[35] Cuts to public childcare and elder care meant that many families reverted to more traditional gender roles in which the women took on more of the burden of unpaid care. Single mothers are often dependent on public services to create value for themselves and their children. They became poorer and were at greater risk of falling into precarious situations in which they were economically dependent on a partner, or destitute, often with long-term consequences for their children.

It is worth mentioning here how DSGE models portray unemployment and unpaid care work. According to these models, there are only two kinds of activities people can do: labour and leisure. When we 'choose' (which of course is completely voluntarily!)

not to work, this is because we believe that our pay is not high enough, and we value our free time more. The models are unable to capture if you are actually unemployed because you have to take care of your children, are sick, have been discriminated against or because a team of economists has recommended that your branch of the healthcare or education sector should be shut down. These models are completely uninterested in everything that takes place outside of the workforce – which to them is just free time. Acknowledging that something valuable takes place in the home would require that the models had a language for the relationship between a child and a parent, or a worker and the rest of their family.[36] But they don't. So, according to a DSGE model, it looks like a bunch of women have just chosen to chill out instead of working after the financial crisis. But many of these women have been acting as unpaid buffers for the care that disappeared.

Back to budget cuts. When people don't receive care, it affects their health and well-being. In Greece, one of the countries that was hit hardest by the financial crisis, the number of severe depressive episodes increased from 3.3 per cent in 2008 to 12.3 per cent in 2013. The rate of suicide in Europe rose after the crisis by 6.5 per cent and even after the economy had technically stabilised, that number did not go back down. Families with adult children with disabilities across Europe said that the conditions for their children were markedly worse in 2016 than they were ten years prior.[37] In 2015, Italy reached the highest death rate among elderly people since the Second World War.[38] Cuts to public sector jobs make people discernibly less optimistic about the future.[39] The foreword of the book *Health in Hard Times*, which deals with the consequences of austerity measures in the UK, reads: 'understanding the extent to which local populations are vulnerable or resilient to the "shocks" of large structural changes such as those recently seen in the UK requires a long-term historical perspective which examines the changing social, economic and physical resources in those areas.'[40] Understanding the human consequences of cuts to care takes a long, long time and a lot of work. Looking at the costs that have been spared, by comparison, is quick and easy.

Still, austerity measures are portrayed as politically neutral by many politicians, journalists and civil servants. For much of the population, economic advice seems like a technical matter, but how a crisis is handled is actually a matter of what economic goals you have.

Austerity demands like those Europe was subject to during the debt crisis in 2010 will be familiar to many people around the globe, particularly in the form of the structural adjustment programmes that the World

Bank has rolled out in some of the world's struggling economies. In 2023, 85 per cent of the world population was subject to these reforms, including 94 so-called developing countries.[41] In IMF's 66-page long overview of their DSGE model, GIMF, the words 'care', 'education' and 'public sector' do not appear once.[42] When care looks like an expense, those who insist on its importance seem economically irresponsible, while those who are against it seem economically responsible. But this isn't the reality.

Some of you might be thinking: but wouldn't everyone have been worse off if we didn't do anything about the debt in 2010? That doesn't seem to be the case. The New Economics Foundation found that the countries 'that pursued greater austerity and cuts to public spending ended up with higher government debt levels.'[43] Who knew – it's actually pretty smart to keep people healthy, happy and alive, even if DSGE models don't see that work as creating anything. It isn't just nice to be cared for. It is also good for the economy. The models fail even on their own terms.

SPECTACULARLY USELESS

Professor emeritus of economics Niels Kærgård writes the following about the dominance of DSGE models based on micro-foundations: 'It is puzzling that the current trend ... seems so unilaterally to be the equilibrium model, even while large swathes of economic front-line research are moving away from these models; away from rational utility and profit maximizing agents in favour of more altruistic, impulse-motivated frameworks.'[44]

And yes. This is puzzling for many, myself included. An entire branch of political economics is dedicated to understanding why exactly these models have gained so much traction. The reasons are multiple and complex. The political economist Oddný Helgadóttir has called DSGE a super-model because it caught on so quickly. She found that equilibrium models made it easier for economists with fewer resources and lower status to be present on the international scene by doing research based on these new models.[45] Microfoundations were good for their careers because they depicted the world as simpler than it actually was, and thus demanded less computing power and money, yet could still give the impression that you were modelling the entire economy.

The models that end up dominating our world aren't chosen by some rigorous, fair competition where the best one wins. It is a power struggle. As we saw with the Koch brothers and the Red Scare, the theory of equilibrium has always been popular among those who had enough money to be able to pay for their own care, and so would rather not pay taxes. And naturally, economists will often tend to defend the models they have dedicated their lives to learning how to use.

A former chief of staff in the Danish Ministry of Finance said that the critique of their DSGE models was reminiscent of Donald Trump's populism and was a sign of 'scepticism about society's core institutions'.[46] Three economists wrote in 2018 that people who rejected DSGE were 'dilettantes' who weren't 'serious about policy analysis'.[47] If you criticise a particular economic model, you're not only a Trumpian populist trying to dismantle the foundations of society, but also incompetent and ignorant. Many feminist economists have been met with this kind of attack whenever they have challenged the existing view of macroeconomics.[48]

It is extremely odd that these critiques are met with such arrogance, particularly considering that it was primarily critics of DSGE who saw the mammoth financial crisis in 2008 coming.[49] And let us not forget that there *is* no agreement in economics about how to use models to portray the world. The Nobel Prize winner Paul Romer wrote in 2016 that macroeconomics had 'gone backwards' for the past 30 years.[50] Another Nobel Prize winner called Paul, this time Krugman, said when it comes to DSGE after the financial crisis, economists should 'admit to [them]selves how very sad the whole story has become.'[51] This was a few years after he called the past decade's macroeconomics 'spectacularly useless at best'.[52] A third Nobel Prize winner, Joseph Stiglitz, wrote in 2018 that the Lucas critique was where 'modern macro went wrong'.[53] (This might also be a fruitful time to mention that the economics Nobel is not an actual Nobel like chemistry or physics. It was invented by the Swedish Riksbank. It literally, like we have seen so many times now, is a mimicry of the natural sciences, made to give economics the sheen of professional authority.)

Little energy is spent sharing this criticism of DSGE with the public, because it reveals that economists are constantly disagreeing with one another and that they, for the most part, have no idea what is going on. In *A Practical Guide to Macroeconomics* (2024), a former employee in the American Federal Reserve, Jeremy B. Rudd, writes that no economist knew there would be a spike in inflation in 2021, or that it would disappear so quickly, and that it is 'embarrassing from a professional standpoint, because it highlights that we still understand close to nothing about how inflation works despite seven decades' worth of research'.[54] Keeping inflation down and understanding financial crises are among the top priorities of established economics, so this is actually pretty embarrassing.[55] But economists don't seem to think it is embarrassing that care work doesn't exist as a prerequisite for life and work in these models at all. Perhaps they should?

Established economics, which, according to Marshall has 'outrun every other branch of the study of man',[56] meets its limit when it comes to something as simple as the fact that people need care in order to exist.

The people who provide care and who have fought for its value have tended to have very little power, both politically and economically. They are, as we'll see, paid very little and receive very little recognition. What can't be measured comes cheap. And the people who have the most acute care needs are usually sidelined by politicians: the poor, the disabled, children. It has taken decades to prove that an economic model without care creates societies that rob people both of the ability to care and to be cared for with dignity.

Still, we are told that DSGE models can be used to assess policies that shape every facet of our lives. This might be why, as the anthropologist David Graeber once said that in our society the rule is: 'the more obviously your work benefits others, the less you're paid for it.'[57]

BEATING HEARTS IN A BROKEN SYSTEM

'The people who began and ran this system were good people who thought of themselves as reformers helping the helpless. But they never asked us what we wanted. Freedom.'

MARK O'BRIEN, *HOW I BECAME A HUMAN BEING*

CHAPTER 9

'Women cost society 12 million kroner during their lives,' proclaimed a headline in the Norwegian online newspaper *Nettavisen*.[1] Now we know what lurks behind this number. In equilibrium models and in GDP, unpaid work is worthless and taxes are always equal to contribution. Globally, the care sector is made up of 248 million women and 132 million men.[2] Women are especially overrepresented on the 'care floor': the lowest-ranking positions that involve direct contact with citizens.[3] And salaries on the floor are low.

Because equilibrium models are unable to calculate the value of anything that isn't available on the market, politicians have held the public sector in increasing suspicion. This suspicion has, over the past 40 years, drastically changed working conditions. Complaints of dwindling productivity have haunted hospital corridors, classrooms and unemployment offices. In 2023, the economist Julian Jessop sang an oft-heard refrain: the 'sluggish' public sector was 'hamstrung' by low productivity, and the first issue he raised was 'lack of competition'.[4] The market, as so often before, is presented as the zenith of efficiency, bringing out the best in people and institutions. The market mimics the natural world; the public care sector, it is professed, should mimic the market.

According to the International Labour Organization (ILO), there is a so-called 'care pay penalty' that means that across the globe, care sector jobs pay 10–40 per cent less relative to jobs that require the same level of education and experience in other sectors.[5] Some theorists go so far as to call care workers 'prisoners of love' because their personal motivation for providing care means that their salaries can be squeezed.[6] In the public care sector in Denmark, the economist Birthe Larsen found that nurses earn 11–17 per cent less than others in comparable positions.[7] Right now, private companies – and indeed, all of society – are getting a pretty good deal on paid care.

When political management tools are unable to describe our care needs as central to a functioning society, it is incredibly easy to cut the services dedicated to those needs. This has serious consequences. The economist Nancy Fraser calls the current global situation a crisis of social reproduction.[8] WHO estimates there will be a shortage of 10 million health workers by 2030, primarily in middle and low income countries.⁹ But the EU predicts that at wealthier latitudes too, care workers will be in short supply in the long term because of 'the sector's ... poor employment terms and conditions compared to other sectors.'[10] In 2021, one in five nurses in Belgium, Canada, France, England and the United States said that they were considering leaving the profession.[11] In England, 40,000 teachers, almost 9 per cent of the entire profession, left their jobs at state schools before retirement between 2021 and 2022.[12]

Partly due to the fact that the value of care is so uncertain, many politicians and economists turned their backs on care investments in the 1990s and 2000s. Care was a large expense, and maybe we could get more for our money. They just needed to figure out how to make care more productive. But what does looking after another person 'produce'?

CALCULATING CARE

Attempts to increase productivity in the public sector using established economic methods have been made in most parts of the world for many decades. In Denmark, cuts of 2 per cent every year were made to the healthcare sector from 1998 to 2018 because it was believed that this corresponded to the average productivity increase in the private sector.[13] Susanne Ekman, associate professor at the Department for Humans and Technology at Roskilde University, has said: 'It is doubtful the extent to which theories of constant increases in efficiency and growth in companies can be translated to the public sector. The public sector is defined by relational tasks that require human contact and interaction.'[14] But this type of increased efficiency is exactly what government ministers have attempted to do.

The creation of value in the public sector is a perpetual source of debate in modern politics. Listening in on this conversation, you would think we had concrete, clear numbers on whether the public sector is running in an optimal way or not. But the truth is that no one really knows.

In 2005, England released a comprehensive report on public sector productivity, the Atkinson Review. Its first principle was that, 'The measurement of government non-market output should, as far as possible, follow a procedure parallel to that adopted in the national accounts for market output.'[15] The aim is always to make care speak the language of the market.

But this is an impossible struggle. Because established economics assumes that market prices correspond most closely to value, you run into a brick wall the moment something isn't available on the market. The World Bank writes: 'The lack of (competitive) market transactions makes it difficult to determine the economic value of a public service, as consumers cannot reveal their valuations through quantities purchased or prices paid.'[16] Based on this, the Danish productivity commission concluded in 2013 that due to this: 'no one can really know how much value the public sector creates.'[17]

If you can't pin down value, can you at least measure how productive care is? If only! Established economics trusts prices so much that they use these to measure productivity. This is why the OECD excludes education, health and care in their overview of productivity among their member countries in 2024; they are all 'non-market' goods, and the OECD doesn't really have any sense of what's happening in those fields.[18] One might think there would be a strong correlation between care, education and productivity, but again – that's all in the clouds.

The World Bank puts it straightforwardly: 'There is no silver bullet for accurately measuring public-sector productivity.'[19] But the anxiety that arises in the system when you don't have any way to measure productivity only increases the demand for a way to calculate it.

In 2004, Mervyn King, the governor of the Bank of England, said the priority for macroeconomics should not be measuring the value of public services but rather measuring all the resources wasted from people not being able to work in the private sector, where there is a market and therefore real value creation.[20] The requirement to find hard numbers somewhere in this black hole sucking value from the 'real economy' has led to reductive measurements. These measurements have had 'perverse consequences', as the economist Richard Boyle once wrote.[21]

A HYPOTHETICAL PERSON

From the 1980s through the 2010s, the *economic style of thinking* was implemented in the public sector. Many politicians, economists and civil servants believed that it was possible to increase efficiency in the public sector by treating it like a company, often taking inspiration from the theories of scientific management that were used in the private sector. One could, according to the so-called public choice theory, use established economic methods to analyse the efficiency in the public sector.

The tendency to use economic metrics to increase efficiency and to 'cost-benefit' analyse the work of public employees goes by many names, but is typically called New Public Management (NPM). I should include a trigger warning here; this method lies at the heart of what many employees and citizens have experienced as a traumatic chain of events.

The political theorists Sandra Dawson and Charlotte Dargie define NPM as a paradigm of public administration from the 1980s and 1990s that held that 'the public and private sectors did not have to be organized and managed in fundamentally different ways. Indeed, that it would be better for the public services if they could be organized and managed as much like the private sector as possible.'[22] This is the culmination of the narrative of this entire book: the tools of economics have infiltrated all aspects of our lives. The citizen has become a product that must be produced as cheaply as possible.

NPM assumes that care providers and care receivers are driven by self-interest. The values that have been associated with the mechanical, competitive market should now 'conquer' the care territory. Because services are not based on competition, it is assumed that time has been wasted and that public sector employees are lazy. NPM therefore contains an inbuilt requirement for efficiency ratings and documented improvements. They need numbers.

The anthropologist Jonathan Gledhill has described this as 'a system of project evaluation in which what is really being evaluated is the procedural efficiency of action in terms of the agency's mission rather than its substantive impact on the lives of human beings.'[23] This results in an institutional culture in which things that can't be economically represented are deemed to be inappropriate or irrelevant, as Michael Power wrote in *The Audit Society*.[24] What can't be measured is represented as inefficient and unscientific. The most important function of the public sector – sending healthy, functional and happy people out into the world – is relegated to the background.

So how are we supposed to know whether we are spending too much or too little? Of course, the economic style of thinking suggests the same thing it has all along: let's invent a fake average person, and hazard a guess at what a service would cost them. We then get an 'average/efficient' set of human needs and a 'cost-intensive/inefficient' set of human needs. This is the exact same approach we saw with Stanley Jevons in the 1870s, when he created a 'hypothetical simplification' by making the main character of his economic theory a civilised English gentleman.

In order to measure efficiency, economists create categories of people and services that can be put into an equation to find an average. These could be called 'product groups'. They might include a hypothetical student, someone who has an alcohol use disorder, someone with a personality disorder or an eating disorder, someone with dyslexia, someone who is neurodivergent, unemployed, elderly or has a gastrointestinal illness.

In the real world these groups are infinitely varied. This is the fundamental difference between products and people: no two people are the same. Every person that needs care is deeply complex and might need wildly different things to reach the same outcome. You cannot set a firm relationship between input and output when it comes to care. Every body and mind requires different inputs to reach the same ouput: being healthy, happy and alive.

There is a huge difference between being unemployed and having an alcohol use disorder and between being unemployed and having a personality disorder. And there is a difference between being a chronically sick student and a student whose parents are refugees. New Public Management is the middle management of macroeconomics. A set of criteria is assembled, far from reality, that seem logical and rational in relation to the goal of efficiency, but when these criteria meet a complex and embodied world, they seem very perverse.

In this method of evaluation, all the processes that don't live up to the average price per citizen or service are deemed to be ineffective and too costly, in need of increased efficiency. Remember that it always counts as a loss the second someone steps foot into the public sector. The social yield of the service for the person is difficult to measure and define, in part because its effects last for the rest of a person's life, and likely also for the lives of their families, children and loved ones. Measuring the price? That's easy. This also makes it increasingly difficult to argue for early interventions in care, as it is impossible to exactly price the future need for care this type of intervention might avoid. Who knows the exact amount saved by a social club for at-risk youths? Who would end up in crime, and who would not? The skewed valuation is staggering. It is as if every effect that cannot be priced in advance hardly gets to exist in the decision-making process.

Care workers struggle to give citizens what they need because that is not strictly the goal of their jobs. The goal is to send someone out the door within the determined resource and time limitations. Many, many people on both sides of the care line have suffered from this over time.

CARE DEBT

This approach concretely impacts the working lives of many care providers. In 2023, OECD reported that across their 38 member countries '57% of hospital physicians and nurses perceived staff levels and work pace to be unsafe.'[25] A study from the University of Belfast from 2015 showed that 73 per cent of English social workers experienced burnout.[26] The same report included an example of what we could probably call a 'prisoner of love'. An anonymous social worker reported: 'My issue is with the department and the torture they put us through, my service users keep me going. The department is forcing me to consider leaving social work as they do not provide quality care to our service users ... they are numbers or targets ... not people.'[27] In Denmark, the Economic Council of the Labour Movement has found that the workplaces with the most cases of burnout are those 'where employees are in close contact with people'.[28] In a survey of over 10,000 respondents in healthcare across Spain and Spanish-speaking countries in South America, 83 per cent said that they 'occasionally' or 'often' made mistakes because of their working conditions.[29] The loss of quality of care for citizens and employees that happens as a result of this situation is practically invisible. It exists in language and lives, while cuts exist in numbers.

Associate professor Susanne Ekman has called this invisible loss of value a 'debt', which, as in the 2008 financial crisis, accumulates until it finally implodes. In her book *Giftig gæld* (Dangerous Debt), she writes that states often 'speculate' about the care debts they owe citizens and kick the can down the road to the next government. The state's economic calculations obscure care needs and this forces public employees to remedy them outside of work hours: 'The so-called "increasing efficiency of the public sector" is often just debt speculation ... that undermines the quality of services, the workplaces and morale of employees.'[30] In the UK a recent so-called 'shake-up' of nursery staffing has left care workers reeling. In 2024, care professionals called for help. They described their work as 'more crowd control than education'. Many said the conditions for two-year-olds were no longer safe. A balanced budget meant unbalanced lives.[31]

Politicians can use the macroeconomic representation of care as worthless to justify cuts and spend this money on something else without seeming like they are depriving their citizens of anything. But of course, the consequences exist in reality. The spaces in which care can happen are constantly shrinking.

In May 2022, 54 per cent of psychologists working in the Danish public sector reported that they 'could not offer patients essential treatments, including psychotherapy and diagnostic re-evaluations because there are not sufficient resources.'[32] Relatedly, the psychologist Maria Holmgaard Secher from Northern Jutland told the Danish newspaper *Politiken*:

> Honestly, the pressure makes it feel like we're working at a Toyota factory. Psychiatry is turning into an assembly line and it isn't doing our patients any good ... We are stuck in this strained system, where you are always trying to do the best you can, but you can see that it is nowhere near enough ... People do extra work in the shadows, run a little faster and bend the rules for their patients, but this isn't feasible in the long run. And our patients are not benefitting from burnt out staff.[33]

Two things stand out. It is not odd that the work feels like a Toyota factory, because that has always been the ideal. Secondly, Secher's approach to her patients fundamentally conflicts with the assumptions of NPM and the economic style of thinking. She is not driven primarily by self-interest, she is driven by doing good by her patients.

CONFLICTING INTERESTS

Since the rise of the economic style of thinking in the 1980s, public employees and citizens have been subject to increasing surveillance and auditing. The assumption at the core of it was that *Homo economicus*, ever thinking of themselves, would abuse the system if not constantly evaluated.

The examples are infinite: economists who try to measure the effectiveness of public school teaching by comparing PISA tests year after year.[34] Municipalities that try to make nursing cheaper by asking people to register precisely how long they spent blowing a patient's nose.[35] Economists that conclude that further investment in the human capital of small children is unwise because it won't result in efficiency gains in other sectors.[36]

There is a constant drive to maximise efficiency and to spend increasingly less time on real care work, because its long-term consequences are the most difficult to measure, and therefore there is a constant suspicion that there is laziness hiding in there. Professor of public administration Steven Van de Walle has shown that NPM paradoxically built a system in which citizens and public employees are cast as having conflicting interests.[37] The scrounging citizen tries to get as much care as they can without paying; the lazy employee tries to do as little as possible. The end result is that constant documentations, audits and evaluations are the only way to trust anyone. It's ironic; a case of attempting to restore public trust by literally creating distrust. When you don't have a language to express that legitimate care needs are a natural part of any economy, every person that seeks care is a cause for suspicion. The absurd consequence of this has been that only efficiency, documentation and constant monitoring in and of themselves become the goal. Today, Danish social workers employed by the offices for children and youth services spend 82 per cent of their collective work time on administration.[38] (The dystopia is here.)

< >

The head of the Danish NGO AskovFonden, Helle Øbo, who has spent many years working with the most under-resourced members of society, writes in her book *Man møder et menneske* (You Meet a Person) that we should focus on what she calls relational welfare: 'A view of human nature in which everyone can and wants to be engaged in their own lives, so long as they are met as a fellow human being and with the assumption that people need to be understood in context. In practice, this means giving employees the freedom to build authentic relationships with the people they are helping.'[39] We will never have this kind of care so long as we have a system that sees a loss of control of every minute as a potential loss of value. There can be great value in things that take time. There can be great value in things you can't put a price on. A slow, patient process might be exactly what is needed to enable the human transformation that care is.

NPM claims to create a system that speaks to the 'true nature' of humans, namely our self-interest, but what actually happens is a regimenting of suspicion, in which those who do trust the system don't get what they need. Those who try to help and provide care with good intentions are punished. The methods create the reality. But other methods create other realities.

In the Netherlands, a nurse called Jos de Blok came up with a new way to provide elder care, called 'neighbourhood care'. The main requirement was that care workers spend a minimum of 61 per cent of their time with the elderly. They would have more freedom and aim to do as little administrative work as possible.[40] The system has, in all its simplicity, been revolutionary. Employees are much happier, and the elderly are very satisfied with the care they receive. The care provided in this case was more expensive per hour, but of a dramatically higher quality. In the long run, it took only half as long to achieve the same health outcomes as standard elder care based on established economic principles. Employees had a high degree of autonomy in how they chose to spend their time.

The consultancy KPMG analysed the strategy and found that 'higher staff morale and motivation has a beneficial effect on the patient experience. At the same time, the active maximization of clinical time and the reduction of non-value activities is a central tenet to achieving better quality at affordable costs. Sadly, this is an overwhelmingly neglected area, especially in the public sector.'[41] It makes you want to laugh. But it also makes you want to cry.

REVERSE ROBIN HOOD

To argue for more autonomy for care workers in a welfare state doesn't mean that we shouldn't make sure that care is provided in a fair and just way. One of the greatest problems in the public care sector around the world is that we are in what is often called a 'reverse Robin Hood' situation. We take from the poorest and give to the richest. If you are privileged and need more care, you will usually get it. Underprivileged citizens tend to use even the free systems much less, even though they tend to be sicker on average and should be using it more. Across the 35 EU member countries, there is a close relationship between underfinanced healthcare systems and bad access for the most vulnerable citizens.[42] As soon as there is no money, and things need to be more efficient, the 'complex' cases are the first to go. This affects life expectancy, even in Denmark, one of the wealthiest and most equal countries in the world. In 1986, the wealthiest 25 per cent of men lived only 5.5 years longer than the poorest 25 per cent of men. Thirty-two years later – in 2018 – the richest men lived ten years longer than the poorest.[43]

These health disparities are a direct result of the economic logic of efficiency. Underprivileged patients often take up more time, have more co-morbidities, need more frequent testing and can have more difficulty completing their courses of treatment. In a system that measures the number of completed treatment plans rather than whether or not patients have gotten the help they need, it usually doesn't pay to spend time on the most under-resourced patients – who probably won't be the ones asking for help in the first place.[44] The privileged patient becomes the 'normal' patient, not because this is what the staff wants, but rather because the whole system is structured to service the 'normal' hypothetical person – a representative agent, as it were.

This means that people who fall outside the norm risk being exposed to massive neglect. This is true everywhere where work involves human bodies and minds.

When a care system loses the ability to embrace the 'abnormal' citizen, the consequences can be fatal. In 2017, Lara Saleem Yousif Al-Jizani died shortly after giving birth in the Swedish city of Kristianstad. She had undergone a C-section with her previous pregnancy and had asked the doctor for the same treatment over and over again but couldn't express herself in Swedish. No interpreter was called. When they removed the placenta, she bled to death. The researcher Annika Esscher from Uppsala University wrote about similar cases in 2014: 'There was a correlation between the higher risk of maternal death and communication problems. In several of the deaths that occurred among women who did not speak Swedish, a professional interpreter had not been used, and this caused delays in diagnosis and treatment that could have prevented tragic outcomes.'[45] In Denmark we have done away with free interpretation services for patients. The Ministry of Health said this would save 2.4 million kroner.[46]

A society can be so stone-hard
That it fuses into a block
A people can be so bone-hard
That life goes into shock

And the heart is all in shadow
And the heart has almost stopped
Till some begin to build
A city as soft as a body

INGER CHRISTENSEN, *IT*

CONCLUSION

We have come across several paradoxes in this book, and now we end with possibly the most important one: on the one hand, care has no value, and on the other, it makes all other work possible. Throughout history we have attempted to 'solve' this paradox most cheaply within (and outside) the bounds of the law. Care work has been done in the home, in slavery, in poorly paid work backed up by racism and discrimination, au pair schemes and other 'migrant solutions', by poorly paid public employees, smuggled behind cultural biases about the feminine touch, multitasking and 'callings'. Care is both impossible to do without and an obstacle to earning money. This is why the state and the private sector can simultaneously demand that we work more and have more children. It is difficult to live a caring life in this paradox.

The devaluation of care hits women in their wallets, their sense of self and their working conditions, but it hits all of society like a punch to the gut.

In established economics, the Scandinavian welfare states are sometimes, with a smirk, called bumblebees. They are big and fat from their public sectors, and no one understands how they can fly, but they do. Self-interested people shouldn't want to work when they have access to unemployment benefits. We shouldn't be so productive when we have so much vacation. We shouldn't be able to afford to give people the free services that we do. Schools that don't have to compete with each other shouldn't be so good. But still, we're buzzing around. This is because value springs from all the places that can't be counted and measured and is harvested in the places that can be. The 'deficit' creates the 'surplus'. This is the paradox we are trapped in.

The mystery we set out to solve in the introduction should be in sharper focus now. We are both earning more and doing worse because we don't have an accepted political language to describe what creates value for us. The only yardstick we have is prices. This makes it enormously difficult to fight for more of everything that is difficult to put a price on. This applies to care, education, friends, leisure, sleep, nature, art, well-being, calm and love. Prices have been backed by many as a scientifically honest approach to value. I don't think they are.

I could easily find an economist who agrees that value is created in the home, in friendships and in the public sector. I also think I could get them to put a price on it. But that wouldn't be in the spirit of this book. It would reduce even more hours of our lives to services that are assigned value based on their relationship to the market. And I don't believe that the market should be the yardstick for everything anymore. Prices mislead, and they lie. They don't tell us what we need to know. There is no apolitical number capable of capturing value. The question of what makes a 'healthy economy' is a democratic one.

We need to use other methods and tools to assess what direction to go in next. The total amount of money in a society doesn't describe the total amount of value, so we can't answer 'can we afford that?' with a yes or a no. Many, many sciences, philosophies and ideologies need to be at play if we are to figure out what futures are possible.

While I've been writing this, I've speculated about a particular *vibe* in politics: it feels as if we have given up entirely on making large, comprehensive political decisions for fear of not being able to put a price on their outcomes.

The only 'right' that politicians can protect with 'precision' is the right to buy more on the market – because the results of this can be measured.

Consequently, the aim of policy is to increase this number. What should be the means to our happiness – money – has become the end in itself. There is no talk of giving us the right to more of what we can't put a number on: vacation days, care for our bodies and minds, education, maybe a society in which no children are poor.

But we ascribe a false 'security' to price-based policy. Knowing the numbers isn't the same as knowing the consequences. A study of 180 political elections across the Western world found that cuts to public services increased political polarisation.[1] Making economic decisions without social considerations doesn't mean that we will stop having feelings, obligations and care needs. We don't become numbers just because we're treated like numbers; we just become unhappy. The Enlightenment thinkers were right that society is like a body. But a body is not mechanical. Feminist economics gives us tools to challenge the prevailing view. There is immense value being created in society that has never been measured. Many of the things we desire – more time with one another, better conditions for those of us in difficulty, childhood, illness, pain or old age – are not expenses. They are expanses, opening up new possibilities and enriching us greatly.

The fear of chaos that we encountered at the start of this book saturates politics. Politicians have tried to systematise the world, as if that would eliminate human fallibility. But as long as the goal is a society with more money in it, there will always be a pull away from those things that are hardest to put a price on, and the people deemed expensive, valueless or immeasurable will face constant degradations. There can be great violence in a spreadsheet.

< >

We do not live in a society where everyone is treated as if they were equally valuable. We live in a society in which your ability to earn money shapes your opportunities and status.

Established economic thinking has contributed to massive injustices, whether or not it meant to. In the pursuit of objective measurements, it has ended up making market hierarchies seem like the result of natural law. And these hierarchies seem 'fair' because the amount of money in someone's bank account is supposed to correspond to their societal value. Graphs and spreadsheets have been so convincing that the conversation about who and what actually creates value has fallen silent. Every attempt to speak about value differently is dismissed as unfounded, unscientific and naïve. As the historian Sheila Rowbotham writes: 'The oppressed without hope are mysteriously quiet. When the conception of change is beyond the limits of the possible, there are no words to articulate discontent so it is sometimes held not to exist.'[2] Established economic methods have colonised every hour of our lives, but worse, they have colonised our minds.

Our entire culture has lost the ability to talk about our need for care and the uncontrollable things that affect us all. We think – like established economists – that perfect planning, optimisation and streamlining of our bodies, minds and careers will mean that we won't need help from other people, that we can protect ourselves from the loss of control, that we can isolate ourselves from the unpredictability of the future. We are therefore rarely able to be accommodating when other people lose their footing. We retreat from sickness, death, grief and violence. We don't want to think that the world isn't systematic and fair. We think that control is the same as happiness, but this is only because we are avoiding the risk of grief instead of actively seeking joy.

This has closed off our future. We are in a preposterous situation where there are infinite technological possibilities and so much money, and yet, it feels as if we have tacitly accepted that humanity's greatest collective achievements in life, equality and happiness lie behind us. It does not have to be this way. Feminist economics shows us not only value, but also another history of humanity. One that is not defined by strife, war and self-interest, but by collaboration and care. These immense parts of who we are have been hidden, shoved into the home, privatised, looked down upon. But they are not the exception, they are the rule.

I feel immense grief. Grief for all the people who have been denied essential care because they didn't fit into the system. Grief for the people who are fighting to provide care in institutions and contexts that don't value it. Grief for a world in which people are told that their preventable suffering is unpreventable.

The methods we use to measure and assess society are in constant conflict with our humanity. When efficiency and productivity are the ideal, then there is only one way to be human. This pulls us towards sameness. Since the Enlightenment we have dreamt of creating a systematic society, and we nearly have. There are only glimpses now of life that doesn't follow a strict schedule. There are only few moments in which care can bring us somewhere beautiful we had not planned.

When I started writing this book, I set out to give you a lens through which to see our society. Many of you have probably been told you would never measure up. You know what I mean when I talk about being perceived as a deficit.

We create so much value for each other. It's difficult to measure, but it isn't difficult to feel.

THANK YOU, THANK YOU, AND THANK YOU TO:

Shëkufe Tadayoni Heiberg and Maya Solovej, who read the earliest versions of these thoughts. That was in 2017. To Malte Frøslee Ibsen, a friend who has given me so many great ideas along the way and faithfully read all my drafts. I owe you a beer. To Jacob Rask, Caspar Eric, Moussa Mchangama, Marie Meyle, Oddný Helgadóttir and Rune Møller Stahl for knowing about the very specific things that you do. The value of specialised knowledge is hard to measure, but when you need it, it's the game in town! To Sofie Winding, who knows that beauty can't be counted but can be felt. Thank you to Line Miller and Nina Zinck at Politikens Forlag, you saw me! And to Sofie Wasenius Mikkelsen for reading so carefully and keeping track of all the sources. The English edition would never have been what it is without Sherilyn Hellberg, who so expertly captured why writing about economics demands the same sensitivity as literature about our innermost lives. Thank you so much to Amanda Waters and the whole team at Ebury, I am honestly thunderstruck by your skill and confidence in me. And my agent, Laurence Laluyaux, who always knows what to do. The author is dead, everything is community.

And last but not least thank you to Eva Eistrup for showing the utmost respect for yourself and your surroundings by being so passionately interested in how the world works. Nothing is more valuable than your time.

And thank you to all of you who have kept me healthy, happy and alive: you haven't just made life possible; you've also made it fun. Thank you.

NOTES

Introduction
1. Torben K. Andersen. 'Kvinder er en underskudsforretning for statskassen.' *Mandag Morgen*, 26 April 2020.
2. Christine Hyldahl. 'Nye tal: Kvinder er en underskudsforretning for samfundet.' *DR Nyheder*, 31 January 2013.
3. Laura Kuenssberg and Joseph Cassidy, 'Reform UK candidate apologises over Hitler neutrality comments.' BBC, 10 June 2024.
4. Caroline Fairchild. 'Paul Krugman: Greg Mankiw Forgets "We Are A Much More Unequal Society Now."' *Huffpost*, 23 June 2013.
5. Diane Coyle. *Cogs and Monsters: What Economics Is, and What It Should Be*. Princeton University Press, 2023, p. 16.
6. Joan Robinson. *Collected Economic Papers*. The MIT Press, 1980, p. 12.
7. Paul Samuelson in the foreword of Philip Saunders' *The Principles of Economics Course: A Handbook for Instructors*. New York: McGraw Hill, 1990.
8. J. Maesse, S. Pühringer, T. Rossier and P. Benz. *The Role of Power in the Social Studies of Economics: An Introduction* in J. Maesse, S. Pühringer, T. Rossier and P. Benz (eds), *Power and Influence of Economists: Contributions to the Social Studies of Economics*. Routledge, 2022, p. 4.
9. Marion Fourcade, Etienne Ollion and Yann Algan. 'The Superiority of Economists', *Journal of Economic Perspectives*. Vol. 29, No. 1, Winter 2015, pp. 89–114.
10. 'Råd og Vismænd.' De Økonomiske Råd.
11. Kenneth Praefke and Kristian Jensen. 'Én ud af 35 af de økonomiske prognoser rammer rigtigt.' *Dagbladet Information*, 14 December 2013.
12. Rachel Treisman. 'JD Vance went viral for "cat lady" comments. The centuries-old trope has a long tail'. *NPR*, 29 July 2024: https://www.npr.org/2024/07/29/nx-s1-5055616/jd-vance-childless-cat-lady-history
13. Jens Bonke and Anders Weise Christensen. *Hvordan bruger danskerne tiden?* Rockwool Fondens Forskningsenhed, 2018.

14 International Labour Organization (ILO). 'Unpaid care work prevents 708 million women from participating in the labour market.' Geneva: ILO, 2024.
15 Jacques Charmes. *The Unpaid Care Work and the Labour Market. An analysis of time use data based on the latest World Compilation of Time-use Surveys.* International Labour Office – Geneva: ILO, 2019, p. 3.
16 Københavns Universitet. 'Det koster kvinder 20 procent på lønnen at få børn.' *Københavns Universitetsnyheder*, 5 March 2018.
17 European Parliament Research Unit. 'What if care work were recognised as a driver of sustainable growth?', 2022.
18 Diversitetsbarometer 2023, Tænketanken EQUALIS. https://equalis.dk/wp-content/uploads/2023/02/Diversitetsbarometeret-2023.pdf
19 Laura Rayner and Danielle Brady. 'Gender Equality: Who Cares? Do You?', European Policy Centre, 8 March 2022.
20 International Labour Organization (ILO). *Care Work and Care Jobs for the Future of Decent Work.* Geneva: ILO, 2018.
21 Michael Franczak and Olúfẹ́mi O. Táíwò. 'Here's how to repay developing nations for colonialism – and fight the climate crisis.' *Guardian*, 14 January 2022.
22 Edward P. Lazear. 'Economic Imperialism', *Quarterly Journal of Economics*. Vol. 115, No. 1, 2020, pp. 99–146.
23 Anne Sørensen. 'Efterkrigstiden 1945–1973: Økonomisk vækst og Velfærdsstaten.' Danmarkshistorien.dk, Aarhus Universitet, 2020.

Chapter 1: A Mechanical Universe
1 Plato. *Phaedo*. Harvard University Press, p. 67.
2 Hans Peter Broedel *Malleus Maleficarum and the construction of witchcraft*. Manchester University Press, 2003, p. 16.
3 Keith Thomas. *Religion and the Decline of Magic*. New York: Scribner, 1971.
4 Carolyn Merchant. *The Death of Nature: Women, Ecology and the Scientific Revolution*. HarperOne, 1990.
5 Silvia Federici. *Caliban og Heksen*. Translated by Emma Holten. Informations Forlag, 2023, p. 337.
6 Frances and Joseph Gies. *Women in the Middle Ages*. Crowell, 1978, p. 228.
7 'Special Eurobarometer 465 – Gender Equality 2017.' The European Union, June 2017. https://data.europa.eu/data/datasets/s2154_87_4_465_eng?locale=en

8 Maria Mies. *Patriarchy and Accumulation on a World Scale: Women in the International Division of Labour*. Zed Books, 2014.
9 Laurent Merceron. 'Gold and Silver Coined from Human Blood.' *Laphams Quarterly*, 16 July 2012.
10 Jean Bodin. *On the Demon-Mania of Witches*. 1580, pp. 6, 53.
11 A.J. Bohrer. 'Sorcery and Sovereignty: Bodin's Political Economy of the Occult.' *Political Theology*, 2020, pp. 479–95.
12 Johannes Overbeek. 'Mercantilism, Physiocracy and Population Theory', *South African Journal of Economics*. Vol. 41, 1973, pp. 108–13.
13 Gunnar Heinsohn and Otto Steiger. 'Inflation and Witchcraft or The Birth of Political Economy: The Case of Jean Bodin Reconsidered', *International Advances in Economics Research*. Vol. 3, No. 2, 1997.
14 H.C. Erik Midelfort. *Witch Hunting in Southwestern Germany 1562–1684: The Social and Intellectual Foundations*. Stanford University Press, 1972.
15 Susan Bordo. *The Flight to Objectivity: Essays on Cartesianism and Culture*. State University of New York Press, 1987.
16 Julie A. Nelson. 'The Study of Choice or the Study of Provisioning? Gender and the Definition of Economics' in Marianne A. Ferber and Julie A. Nelson. *Beyond Economic Man: Feminist Theory and Economics*. University of Chicago Press, 1993, pp. 23–36.
17 Thomas Hobbes. *Leviathan*. 1651, 'Introduction'.
18 René Descartes. *Traité de L'Homme*, 1664.
19 Elizabeth Fee. 'Women's Nature and Scientific Objectivity' in *Women's Nature: Rationalizations of Inequality*. New York: Pergamon Press, 1983, p. 12.
20 Gaby Mahlberg. 'The Parliament of Women and the Restoration Crisis' in *Democracy and Anti-democracy in Early Modern England 1603–1689*. Brill, 2019.
21 Ina Praetorius. 'The Care Centered Economy: Rediscovering What Has Been Taken for Granted.' *Heinrich Böll Stiftung: Publication Series on Economic and Social Issues*, Vol. 16, 2015.
22 Edmund Chapman. *A Treatise on the Improvement of Midwifery*. London: John Brindly & J. Hodges, 1753, p. v.
23 Elizabeth Nihell. *A Treatise on the Art of Midwifery*. London: A. Morley, 1760, p. 85.
24 Lisa Forman Cody. 'The Politics of Reproduction: From Midwives' Alternative Public Sphere to the Public Spectacle of

Man-Midwifery', *Eighteenth-Century Studies*. Vol. 32, No. 4, 1999, pp. 477–95.
25 Maggie Rose Berke. 'Naturalized Women and Women and Womanized Earth: Connecting the Journeys of Womanhood and the Earth, from the Early Modern Era to the Industrial Revolution.' Senior Projects Spring 2017, Bard College, 2017.
26 Lisa Forman Cody. 'The Politics of Reproduction: From Midwives' Alternative Public Sphere to the Public Spectacle of Man-Midwifery', *Eighteenth-Century Studies*. Vol. 32, No. 4, 1999, pp. 477–95.
27 Louis Lapeyre. *An Enquiry into the Merits of These Two Important Questions*. London, 1772, p. 34.
28 For a discussion of Carolyn Merchant's *The Death of Nature*, I would recommend 'Secrets of Nature: The Bacon Debates Revisited', *Journal of the History of Ideas*. Vol. 69, No. 1, 2008, pp. 147–62.
29 Cotton Mather. *Diary of Cotton Mather 1681–1708*. Boston: The Society, 1911, p. 357.
30 Marcelle Mistre Welch and Vivian Bosley. 'On the Equality of the Two Sexes: A Physical and Moral Discourse Which Shows the Importance of Getting Rid of One's Prejudices' in *Three Cartesian Feminist Treaties*. University of Chicago Press, 2002.
31 Eduard Jan Dijksterhuis. *The Mechanization of the World Picture*. Oxford University Press, 1961, p. 357.
32 Moira Ferguson. *First Feminists: British Women Writers, 1578–1799*. Indiana University Press, 1985, pp. 259–60.

Chapter 2: Who Gets to be Free?
1 Thomas Hobbes. *The Collected Works of Thomas Hobbes*. Routledge, 1992, p. 3.
2 Thomas Hobbes, *De Cive (On the Citizen)*. London, 1642, Ch. VIII, p. 10.
3 For an explanation of Hobbes' various perspectives, see: Joanne Boucher. 'Male Power and Contract Theory: Hobbes and Locke in Carole Pateman's "The Sexual Contract"'. *Canadian Journal of Political Science*. Vol. 36, No. 1, 2003.
4 Mary Astell. 'A Prefatory Discourse to Dr. D'Avenant.' *Moderation Truly Stated*. London: R. Wilkin, 1704.
5 Chris Nyland. *John Locke and the Social Position of Women*. University of Wollongong, 1990.
6 John Locke. *Two Treatises of Government*. London: Awnsham

Churchill, 1689. Here, I'm leaning on Nancy Folbre's discussion in *Greed, Lust and Gender*.
7 François Poulain de la Barre. *The Equality of the Sexes*. Manchester University Press, 1990, p. 80.
8 Nancy Folbre. *Greed, Lust and Gender: A History of Economic Ideas*. Oxford University Press, 2009.
9 Johan Olsthoorn and Laurens Van Apeldoorn. '"This man is my property": Slavery and political absolutism in Locke and the classical social contract tradition', *European Journal of Political Theory*. Vol. 21, No. 2, 2022, pp. 253–75.
10 Charles Horton Cooley. *Human Nature and the Social Order* (revised edition). Charles Scribner's Sons, 1922, p. 208.
11 Esme Fuller Thomson, Keri J. West, Joanne Sulman and Stephanie L. Baird. 'Childhood Maltreatment Is Associated with Ulcerative Colitis but Not Crohn's Disease: Findings from a Population-based Study', *Inflammatory Bowel Diseases*. Vol. 21, No. 11, 2015, pp. 2640–8.
12 Sisonke Msimang. 'To be a black mother is to manage the rage of others while growing joyous black children. This is no easy task.' *Guardian*, 8 August 2020.
13 Stanford Encyclopedia of Philosophy, 'Positive and Negative Liberty.'
14 Isaiah Berlin. 'Two Concepts of Liberty' in *Four Essays on Liberty*. Oxford University Press, 1959.
15 Seyla Benhabib. 'The Generalized and the Concrete Other' in *Situating the Self*. Routledge, 1992.
16 Michael Hathaway and Willoughby Arévalo. 'How do fungi communicate?', *MIT Technology Review*, 24 April 2023.

Chapter 3: Through the Eye of a Needle
1 Adam Smith. *The Wealth of Nations with an Introduction by Max Lerner*. The Modern Library, 1937, p. vi.
2 Michele Pujol. *Feminism and Anti-feminism in Early Economic Thought*. Brookfield: E. Elgar, 1992.
3 Adam Smith, *An Inquiry into the Nature and Cause of The Wealth of Nations, Book I*. Chicago: The University of Chicago Press, 1976, p. 89.
4 Sumitra Shah. 'Sexual division of labour in Adam Smith's work', *Journal of the History of Economic Thought*. Vol. 28, No. 2, 2006, pp. 221–41; 228.

5   Adam Smith. *The Wealth of Nations with an Introduction by Max Lerner*. The Modern Library, 1937, p. 14.
6   Emma Rothschild. 'Adam Smith and the Invisible Hand', *American Economic Review*. Vol. 84, No. 2, 1994.
7   Adam Smith. *Teorien om de moralske følelser*. Translated by Claus Bratt Østergaard. Dagbladet Information, 2014, pp. 238, 1, 78.
8   Ian Simpson Ross. *The Life of Adam Smith*. Oxford University Press, 1995, pp. 139–361.
9   Deirdre Nansen McCloskey. 'Adam Smith Did Humanomics: So Should We', *Eastern Economic Journal*. Vol. 42, 2016, pp. 503–13.
10 Adam Smith, *The Theory of Moral Sentiments*. Cambridge University Press, 2002, p. 11, on Loveliness: Chapter 3, part 2, 1.
11 Adam Smith Institute (ASI). 'About Adam Smith.' ASI, n.d., https://www.adamsmith.org, accessed August 2024.
12 Seyla Benhabib. *Situating the Self*. Routledge, 1992, p. 83.
13 Glory M. Liu. *Adam Smith's America: How a Scottish Philosopher Became an Icon of American Capitalism*. Princeton University Press, 2022, p. 192.
14 David Graeber. *The Utopia of Rules: On Technology, Stupidity, and the Secret Joys of Bureaucracy*. Melville House, 2015, p. 40.
15 Paul Krugman. 'The Pin Factory Mystery.' *New York Times*, 2006.
16 Şule Özler. 'Adam Smith and Dependency', *Psychoanalytical Review*. Vol. 99, No. 3, 2012, pp. 333–58.
17 Samira Ariadad. 'The Alien Anorexic and Post-Human Bodies' in *You Must Make Your Death Public*. Mute Books, 2015, p. 49.

Chapter 4: What are We Worth?

1   Edmund Burke. *Thoughts and Details on Scarcity*. 1795, p. 34.
2   W.S. Jevons. *Principles of Science*. 1847 (1905), pp. 735–6.
3   For an exhaustive account of how the marginalists were inspired by physics, I can recommend Philip Mirowski. *More Heat Than Light*. Cambridge University Press, 1989.
4   Alfred Marshall. *Principles of Economics*. Macmillan and Co, 1920, I.II.1
5   Keehyun Hong. 'Professionalization and the Spread of Marginalist Economics in the United States', *Kyoto Economic Review*. Vol. 77, No. 2, 2008, pp. 127–55.
6   Mariana Mazzucato. *The Value of Everything: Making and Taking in the Global Economy*. New York: Public Affairs, 2018, p. 65.
7   Philip Pilkington. 'Deconstructing Marginalist Microeconomics' in *The Reformation in Economics*. Palgrave Macmillan, 2016.

8   Frank H. Knight. *Risk, Uncertainty and Profit*. Cambridge, MA: The Riverside Press, 1921, pp. 374–5. A nod is due here to Nancy Folbre. *The Rise and Decline of Patriarchal Systems: An Intersectional Political Economy*. Verso, 2020, where I found the quote from Knight.
9   Mary Ann Dimand, Robert William Diman and Evelyn L. Forget. *Women of Value: Feminist Essays on the History of Women in Economics*. E. Elgar, 1995.
10 Branko Milanović. *Visions of Inequality: from the French revolution to the end of the Cold War*. Belknap Press, 2023, p. 221.
11 William Thompson (and Anna Wheeler). *Appeal of One Half of the Human Race, Women, Against the Pretensions of the Other Half, Men to Retain them in Political and thence in Civil and Domestic Slavery*. 1825, p. 198.
12 Léon Walras. *Elements of Pure Economics: Or the Theory of Social Wealth*. 1874, p. 69.
13 Andrés Álvarez. 'Léon Walras on Industrial Regulation: Railroads as Economic and Moral State Monopolies', *SSRN Electronic Journal*. 2010.
14 Interview, *This Week*. Thames TV, 5 February 1976.
15 Eilis Lawlor, Helen Kersley and Susan Steed. 'A Bit Rich: Calculating the real value to society of different professions.' New Economics Foundation, 14 December 2009.
16 Kenneth J. Arrow and Gérard Debreu. 'Existence of an Equilibrium for a Competitive Economy', *Econometrica*. Vol. 22, No. 3, 1954, pp. 265–90.
17 Ashley V. Whillans, Elizabeth W. Dunn, Paul Smeets and Michael I. Norton. 'Buying Time Promotes Happiness.' *PNAS*, Vol. 114, No. 32, 2017, pp. 8523–7.
18 'The Future of Luxury.' TLGG Agency, 24 August 2021.
19 Paul A. Samuelson and William Nordhaus. *Economics: An Introductory Analysis* (Paperback – International Edition). McGraw-Hill Education, 1995, p. 88.
20 Robert Skidelsky. *What's Wrong with Economics: A Primer for the Perplexed*. Yale University Press, 2020, p. 27.
21 W. Stanley Jevons. *The Principles of Science*. London: Macmillan, 1874, p. 363. A deeper analysis of his relationship to colonialism can be found in Philip Steer. 'Gold and Greater Britain: Jevons, Trollope, and Settler Colonialism', *Victorian Studies*. Vol. 58, No. 3, 2016.
22 Stephan Pühringer and Lukas Bäuerle. 'What Economics Education Is Missing: The Real World', *International Journal of Social Economics*. Vol. 46, No. 8, 2019, pp. 977–91.

23 Nancy Folbre. 'The Unproductive Housewife: Her Evolution in Nineteenth Century Economic Thought', *Signs*. Vol. 16, No. 3, 1991, pp. 463–84.
24 Mary Ann Dimand, Robert William Diman and Evelyn L. Forget. *Women of Value: Feminist Essays on the History of Women in Economics*. E. Elgar, 1995.
25 Julie A. Nelson. *Feminism, Objectivity, and Economics*. Routledge, 1995, p. xii.
26 Mark Townsend and Michael Savage. 'Fury as Braverman depicts homelessness as a "lifestyle choice".' *Guardian*, 4 November 2023.
27 Lourdes Benería. *Gender, Development and Globalization: Economics as if All People Mattered*. Routledge, 2003.
28 Maddalena Ronchi and Nina Smith. *Daddy's girl: Daughters, managerial decisions, and gender inequality*. 2021, Job market paper.
29 William Moore Gorman. 'Community Preference Fields', *Econometrica*. Vol. 21, No. 1, 1953, pp. 63–80.
30 Isabella Weber and Evan Wasner. 'Sellers' inflation, profits and conflict: why can large firms hike prices in an emergency?', *Review of Keynesian Economics*. 14 April 2023, pp. 183–213.
31 Jonathan Schlefer. *The Assumptions Economists Make*. Belknap Press, 2017.
32 Frank Ackerman and Lisa Heinzerling. 'Pricing the Priceless: Cost-Benefit Analysis of Environmental Protection', *University of Pennsylvania Law Review*. Vol. 150, 2002, pp. 1553–84; Frank Ackerman. 'Still dead after all these years: interpreting the failure of general equilibrium theory', *Journal of Economic Methodology*. Vol. 9, No. 2, 2002, p. 124.
33 Allan Kirman. 'The Intrinsic Limits of Modern Economic Theory: The Emperor Has No Clothes', *Economic Journal*. Vol. 99, 1989.
34 John Komlos. 'Need for a paradigm shift in econ 101.' *Huffington Post*, 11 August 2014.
35 Simon Nyborg. 'Hvad siger du nu, professor?', *Berlingske Tidende*, 12 July 2007.
36 Tim Besley and Peter Hennessy. 'Letter to the Queen', *British Academy Review*. Issue 14, 2009.
37 Kenneth Praefke and Kristian Jensen. 'Én ud af 35 af de økonomiske prognoser rammer rigtigt.' *Dagbladet Information*, 14 December 2013.
38 Lærke Cramon. 'At få småbørn i tøjet burde være 75 kroner værd. Vi har regnet på, hvad kvinders ulønnede arbejde er værd i kroner og øre.' *Dagbladet Information*, 25 June 2022.

Chapter 5: Worthless Maintenance

1. Ritzau. 'Finansministeriet: Afskaffelse af store bededag polstrer statskassen med 3 mia. Kr.' *Børsen*, 11 January 2023.
2. Per Thiemann. 'Det er højst usædvanligt: "Overvismand studser over regeringens regnestykke."' *Politiken*, 9 January 2023.
3. Heinz D. Kurz. 'Two Critics of Marginalist Theory: Piero Sraffa and John Maynard Keynes', *Investigación Económica*. Vol. 71, No. 280, 2012.
4. Ted Winslow. *Keynes's Economics: A Political Economy as Moral Science Approach to Macroeconomics and Macroeconomic Policy*. York University, 2005.
5. M. Guglielmo. 'The Contribution of Economists to Military Intelligence During World War II', *Journal of Economic History*. Vol. 68, No. 1, 2008, pp. 109–50.
6. Paul Samuelson, 'Unemployment ahead: a warning to the Washington expert.' *New Republic*, 11 September 1944, pp. 297–9.
7. Irene van Staveren. 'Post-Keynesianism Meets Feminist Economics', *Cambridge Journal of Economics*. Vol. 34, No. 6, 2010, pp. 1123–44.
8. United Nations (UN), OECD, IMF, World Bank and European Commission. *System of National Accounts 2008*. New York: UN, 2009.
9. Mariana Mazzucato. *The Value of Everything: Making and Taking in the Global Economy*. New York: Public Affairs, 2018, p. 90.
10. Chester Dawson and Jason Dean. 'Rising China Bests a Shrinking Japan.' *Wall Street Journal*, 14 February 2011.
11. Lorenzo Fioramonti. 'A PostGDP World.' *Foreign Policy*, 2 June 2015.
12. Simon Kuznets. 'How To Judge Quality.' *New Republic*, 1962, p. 29.
13. Timothy Mitchell. *Colonizing Egypt*. Cambridge University Press, 1988.
14. Luke Messac. 'Outside the Economy: Women's Work and Feminist Economics in the Construction of National Income Accounting', *Journal of Imperial and Commonwealth History*. Vol. 46, No. 3, 2018, pp. 552–78.
15. Frederick Cooper. *Africa since 1940: The Past of the Present*. Cambridge University Press, 2002.
16. Richard Stone and Giovanna Stone. *National Income and Expenditure*. Bowes and Bowes, 1966, pp. 30–1.
17. Diane Coyle. *GDP: A Brief but Affectionate History*. Princeton University Press, 2014, p. vii.

18 Katie Allen. 'Accounting for drugs and prostitution to help push UK economy up by £65bn.' *Guardian*, 10 June 2014.
19 Wolfgang Streeck. 'The politics of public debt: Neoliberalism, capitalist development, and the restructuring of the state.' MPIfG Discussion Paper, No. 13/7, Max Planck Institute for the Study of Societies, 2013.
20 *Dansk Økonomi, forår 2010* [Economic report]. De Økonomiske Råd, 2010.
21 Finansministeriet: Erfaringer med budgetloven 2014–2020. April 2022, p. 11.
22 International Trade Union Confederation. 'Investing in the Care Economy.' 2016, p. 12.
23 Jacques Charmes. *The Unpaid Care Work and the Labour Market. An analysis of time use data based on the latest World Compilation of Time-use Surveys*. International Labour Office – Geneva: ILO, 2019, p. 3.
24 Hannà Sigga Madslund. 'Sofa på recept til stressede kvinder.' Det nationale Forskningscenter for Arbejdsmiljø, 14 October 2015.
25 John Locke. *Two Treatises of Government*. London: Awnsham Churchill, 1689. Quoted and analysed by Nancy Folbre in *Greed, Lust and Gender*.
26 Tithi Bhattacharya. 'Three Ways a Green New Deal Can Promote Life Over Capital.' *Jacobin*, 10 June 2019.
27 Trucost PLC. *Natural Capital at Risk: The Top 100 Externalities of Business*. Trucost PLC, 2013.
28 Københavns Universitet. 'Grønt gennembrud: Nye regnemaskiner sætter tal på vores natur og klimaaftryk.' *Via Ritzau*, 27 January 2023.
29 Peter Birch Sørensen et al. 'Vandmiljø og Lærkesang.' *Dagbladet Information*, 21 December 2004.
30 Erik Gómez-Baggethun and Roldan Muradian. 'In markets we trust? Setting the boundaries of Market-Based Instruments in ecosystem services governance', *Ecological Economics*. Vol. 117, September 2015, pp. 217–24.
31 Søren Bøye Olsen, Jacob Ladenburg, Mads Lyngby Petersen, Ulrich Lopdrup, Anja Skjoldborg Hansen and Alex Dubgaard. *Motorways versus Nature: A Welfare Economic Valuation of Impacts*. Institut for Miljøvurdering, 2005, p. 3.
32 Vibeke Lyngklip Svansø. 'Topchefer i spidsen for krav om ny grundlov: "Det er vores pligt over for fremtidige generationer."' *Berlingske*, 1 December 2019.

33 Christian Bjørnskov. 'Grøn grundlov – er det virkelig en god idé?', punditokraterne.dk, 2 December 2019.
34 For an economic take on how unpaid care work could be added to macroeconomics, see: Srinivas Raghavendra. 'At the intersection between Class and Gender: Unpaid care work and Macroeconomic demand regimes', 12 December, 2023: https://papers.ssrn.com/sol3/papers.cfm?abstract_id=4738503
35 Johanna Varjonen and Kristiina Aalto. *Household Production and Consumption in Finland 2001.* Household Satellite Account, 2006.
36 Chris S. Payne and Gueorguie Vassilev. *Household Satellite Account, UK: 2015 and 2016.* Office for National Statistics, 2018.
37 Amy Finkelstein, Matthew J. Notowidigdo, Frank Schilbach and Jonathan Zhang. 'Lives vs. Livelihoods: The Impact of the Great Recession on Mortality and Welfare', National Bureau of Economic Research. Working Paper 32110, February 2024.
38 Lola Woetzel et al. 'How advancing women's equality can add $12 trillion to global growth.' McKinsey Global Institute, McKinsey & Company, 1 September 2015.
39 'Women, Employment and Earnings: A pre-budget briefing from the UK.' From Women's Budget Group, March 2020.
40 'Women more likely to have worked part-time in Q3 2023.' Eurostat, 7 March 2023.
41 Brancheorganisationen pensions og forsikringsselskaber (F&P). 'Dobbelt så mange kvinder arbejder deltid efter første barn.' F&P, 14 September 2023.
42 Census 2021: Families and the labour market, UK: https://www.ons.gov.uk/employmentandlabourmarket/peopleinwork/employmentandemployeetypes/articles/familiesandthelabourmarketengland/2021
43 Sophie Holme Andersen and Troels Lund Jensen. 'Working hours among Danish families with children are higher than in most other Western EU countries.' The Economic Council of the Labour Movement, 18 September 2023: www.ae.dk/analyse/2023-09-arbejdstiden-blandt-danske-boernefamilier-er-hoejere-end-i-de-fleste-andre-vestlige
44 Alison Andrew, Oriana Bandiera, Monica Costa Dias, Camille Landais. 'The careers and time use of mothers and fathers.' The Institute for Fiscal Studies, 2021, p. 4.
45 UK Government: Census 2021. Families and the labour market.
46 Anders Borup Christensen. 'Stort potentiale ved lavere sygefravær og flere på fuldtid i det offentlige' [Debatindlæg].

Dansk Arbejdsgiverforening, 13 January 2023: https://www.da.dk/politik-og-analyser/arbejdsmiljoe-og-sundhed/2024/stort-potentiale-i-at-nedbringe-det-offentlige-sygefravaer/#:~:text=Potentiale%20p%C3%A5%20mange%20tusinde%20fuldtidsbesk%C3%A6ftigede&text=I%202022%20var%20det%20et,p%C3%A5%20tv%C3%A6rs%20af%20sektor%2C%20jf

47 Digitaliserings og ligestillingsministeriet. 'Ligestillingsredegørelser 2023.' Digitaliserings- og ligestillingsministeriet, 20 December 2023.

48 Digitaliserings og ligestillingsministeriet. 'Ligestillingsredegørelser 2023.' Digitaliserings- og ligestillingsministeriet, 20 December 2023.

49 Steve Doughty. 'Women take more sick leave then men – but it's usually to look after the kids, official figures show.' *Daily Mail*, 6 October 2015.

50 Marie Bille. 'Ny undersøgelse: Forældre sender syge børn i daginstitution.' BUPL, 22 September 2021: https://bupl.dk/boern-unge/nyheder/ny-undersoegelse-foraeldre-sender-syge-boern-i-daginstitution

51 Bouree Lamb. 'Who Stays Home When the Kids Are Sick?' *Atlantic*, 28 October 2014.

52 Usha Ranji and Alina Salganicoff. 'Balancing on Shaky Ground: Women, Work and Family Health' [Data Note]. Kaiser Family Foundation, 20 October 2014.

53 Nancy Folbre, Laila Gautham and Kristin Smith. 'Essential Workers and Care Penalties in the United States', *Feminist Economics*. Vol. 27, Nos 1–2, 2020, pp. 173–87.

54 Campbell Robertson and Robert Gebeloff. 'How Millions of Women Became the Most Essential Workers in America.' *New York Times*, 18 April 2020.

55 Georgina Phillips et al. 'Women on the frontline: exploring the gendered experience for Pacific healthcare workers during the COVID-19 pandemic', *Lancet*. Vol. 42, 2024.

56 Nina Ausum Agergaard. 'Hvor ofte er det normalt, at små børn bliver syge?' *Samvirke*, 14 July 2022.

57 Carl Cederström. *State of Nordic Fathers*. Nordic Council of Ministers, 2019, p. 14.

58 Rebecca Solnit. 'Nobody Knows.' *Harper's Magazine*, March 2018.

59 Selma James and Mariarosa Della Costa. *The Power of Women and the Subversion of Community*. Falling Wall Press Limited, 1975.

60 Carlos Alberto Duque Garcia. 'Unpaid Housework and

Superexploitation of Labor: A Suggested Model and Empirical Evidence from Mexico and Colombia', *Review of Social Economy*. Vol. 81, No. 4, 2023, pp. 549–73.
61 Louise Toupin. *Wages for Housework: A History of an International Feminist Movement, 1972–77*. Pluto Books, 2018.
62 Rebecca Sear. 'The male breadwinner nuclear family is not the "traditional" human family, and promotion of this myth may have adverse health consequences', *Philosophical Transactions of the Royal Society B*. Vol. 376, 2021.
63 WHO. 'Maternal Mortality.' 26 April 2024: https://www.who.int/news-room/fact-sheets/detail/maternal-mortality
64 Chloe Kim. 'US maternal deaths doubled in last 20 years, study finds.' BBC, 4 July, 2023.
65 'Who takes care of children, household and the elderly? A dossier on the societal dimension of a private question.' German Federal Ministry for Family Affairs, Senior Citizens, Women and Youth, 2020, p. 28.
66 'Global fertility has collapsed, with profound economic consequences.' *Economist*, 1 June 2023.
67 Indenrigs- og Sundhedsministeriets pressevagt. 'Ny aftale sikrer ufrivilligt barnløse gratis hjælp til barn nummer to', 18 June 2024.
68 Indenrigs- og sundhedsministeriet. 'Tidsbegrænsning på nedfrysning af kvinders æg ophæves.' Regeringen, 31 May 2023.
69 Indenrigs- og Sundhedsministeriets pressevagt. 'Ny aftale: Par bestående af to kvinder får lettere hjælp til ægdonation', 31 January 2024.
70 Christopher Livesay. 'Italian Fertility Campaign To Boost National Birth Rate Backfires.' NPR, 1 September 2016.
71 Sian Cain. 'Women are happier without children or a spouse, says happiness expert.' *Guardian*, 25 May 2019.
72 Paul Dolan. *Happy Ever After: Escaping the Myth of the Perfect Life*. Allen Lane, 2019.

Chapter 6: Power Struggles
1 Carl Wittman. *Refugees from Amerika: A Gay Manifesto*. The Red Butterfly, 1970, p. 4.
2 bell hooks. *Feminist Theory: From Margin to Center*. South End Press, 1984, p. 85.
3 Susan Ferguson. *Women and Work: Feminism, Labour, and Social Reproduction*. Between the Lines, 2019.

4. Jonathan M. Metzl. '"Mother's Little Helper" – The Crisis of Psychoanalysis and the Miltown Resolution', *Gender and History*. Vol. 15, No. 2, 2003, pp. 228–55.
5. Daniel Horowitz. 'Rethinking Betty Friedan and The Feminine Mystique: Labour Union Radicalism and Feminism in Cold War America', *American Quarterly*. Vol. 48, No. 1, 1996, pp. 1–42; 22.
6. Gerda Lerner's letters can be found here: Eileen Boris and Elizabeth Currans. 'Reflections', *Frontiers: A Journal of Women Studies*. Vol. 36, No. 1, 2015, pp. 27–32.
7. David J. Garrow. 'The FBI and Martin Luther King.' *Atlantic*, August 2022.
8. Brandt Weathers. 'Lucas Critique After the Crisis: A Historicization and Review of one Theory's Eminence', *New School Economic Review*. Vol. 7, 2012, pp. 3–21.
9. Wolfram Elsner, Torsten Heinrich and Henning Schwardt. *The Microeconomics of Complex Economies Evolutionary, Institutional, and Complexity Perspectives*. Academic Press, 2015, section 12.8.2.
10. Zachary D. Carter. *The Price of Peace: Money, Democracy, and the Life of John Maynard Keynes*. Random House, 2020, p. 379.
11. Christina Wilkie and Joy Resmovits. 'Koch High: How the Koch Brothers Are Buying Their Way Into the Minds of Public School Students.' *Huffpost*, 16 July 2014.
12. bell hooks. *Ain't I a Woman? Black Women and Feminism*. South End Press, 1981, pp. 193–4.
13. Louis Menand. 'Books as Bombs.' *The New Yorker*, 16 January 2011.
14. Ida Zander Jensen. '1000 sosuhjælpere fra tredjelande skal til Danmark.' *TV2*, 24 January 2024.
15. Paula England. 'The Separative Self: Androcentric Bias in Neoclassical Assumptions' in Marianne A. Ferber and Julie A. Nelson. *Beyond Economic Man: Feminist Theory and Economics*. University of Chicago Press, 1993, pp. 38.
16. Cinzia Arruzza, Nancy Fraser and Tithi Bhattacharya. *Feminism for the 99%: A Manifesto*. Verso, 2019, p. 13.
17. Evelyn Nakano Glenn. 'Racial Ethnic Women's Labor: The Intersection of Race, Gender and Class Oppression', *Review of Radical Political Economics*. Vol. 17, No. 3, 1985, p. 86–108.
18. Angela Y. Davis. *Kvinder, race og klasse*. Translated by Mikas Lang. Informations Forlag, 2022.
19. Elizabeth Martinez. *De Colores Means All of Us: Latina Views for a Multi-Colored Century*. South End Press, 1998, p. 488.

20 Cecilia A. Conrad. 'Racial Trends in Labor Market Access and Wages:' Women' in Neil J. Smelser, William Julius Wilson and Faith Mitchell. *America Becoming: Racial Trends and Their Consequences (Vol. 2)*. National Research Council, 2001.
21 Gabriella Rose Beckles-Raymond. 'Revisiting the Home as a Site of Freedom and Resistance' in Akwugo Emejulu and Francesca Sobande. *To Exist is to Resist: Black feminism in Europe*. Pluto Press, 2019, p. 96.
22 Søren Langelund. 'Jeg tog kun to ugers barsel med mine piger. Det er en af mine største fortrydelser.' *Femina*, 21 September 2021.
23 Selma James and Mariarosa Della Costa. *The Power of Women and the Subversion of Community*. Falling Wall Press Limited, 1975, p. 18.
24 Katja Brandt Andersen. 'Aftale på plads: Børn fra ghettoer skal tvinges i institution.' *TV2*, 28 May 2018.
25 'Undskyldning til de 22 grønlandske børn, som blev sendt til Danmark i 1951.' Statsministeriet, 8 December 2020.
26 Jennifer Leason, 'Forced and coerced sterilization of Indigenous women: Strengths to build upon', *Canadian Family Physician*. Vol. 67, No. 7, 2021, pp. 525–7.
27 Angela Y. Davis. *Kvinder, race og klasse*. Translated by Mikas Lang. Informations Forlag, 2022, p. 16.
28 'Arbejdsstyrken fordelt på køn, 1960–1991.' Located on Kvinfo's website under 'Kilde 156'. Ligestillingsrådet, 1992.
29 Anette Borchorst. *Kvinderne, Velfærdsstaten og Omsorgsarbejdet*. Politica, 1989.
30 Arlie Hochschild and Anne Machung. *The Second Shift: Working Parents and the Revolution at Home*. Viking, 1989, p. 1.
31 Henriette Tolstrup Holmegaard and Bjørn Friis Johannsen. 'Science Talent and Unlimited Devotion: An Investigation of the Dynamics of University Students' Science Identities Through the Lens of Gendered Conceptualisations of Talent' in Henriette Tolstrup and Louise Archer (eds). *Science Identities: Theory, method and research* from the series Contributions from Science Education Research, Vol. 12, 2022, p. 126.
32 Brittany Wong. '"Weaponized Incompetence" Screws Women Over at Work and in Relationships.' *Huffpost*, 26 January 2022.
33 Carl Cederström. *State of Nordic Fathers*. Nordic Council of Ministers, 2019.

34 'Undersøgelse blandt forældre til børn med handicap eller kronisk sygdom – deres samarbejde med kommunen og tilknytning til arbejdsmarkedet.' For Lige Vilkår, 2019.
35 Paola Di Giulio, Dimiter Philipov and Ina Jaschinski. 'Families with disabled children in different European countries.' Families and Societies working paper series, 2014, p. 15.
36 Leah Ruppanner. 'Kvinder er ikke bedre til at multitaske end mænd – de laver bare mere.' Videnskab.dk, 23 August 2019.
37 Alex Hern. 'Netflix's biggest competitor? Sleep.' *Guardian*, 18 April 2017.
38 Bronnie Ware. *The Top Five Regrets of the Dying: A Life Transformed by the Dearly Departing*. Hay House Ltd, 2019.

Chapter 7: Isolated Optimisation
1 John Bates Clark. *The Distribution of Wealth: A Theory of Wages, Interest and Profits*. New York: Macmillan Company, 1899, p. 5.
2 Paul Krugman. 'Is the Vibecession Finally Coming to an End?' *New York Times*, 22 January 2024.
3 Sarah Johnson. 'WHO declares loneliness a global public health concern.' *Guardian*, 16 November 2023.
4 Jonas Van der Slycken and Brent Bleys. 'Is Europe Faring Well with Growth? Evidence From a Welfare Comparison in the EU-15 (1995–2018)', *Ecological Economics*. Vol. 217, 2024.
5 Stine Schramm et al. *Sygdomsbyrden i Danmark – risikofaktorer*. Sundhedsstyrelsen, 2022.
6 Andrew Moose and Ruma Bhargawa. 'A generation adrift: Why young people are less happy and what we can do about it.' World Economic Forum, 5 April 2024.
7 Wendy Brown. *Undoing the Demos: Neoliberalism's Stealth Revolution*. Zone Books, 2015.
8 Karl Polanyi. *The Great Transformation: The Political and Economic Origins of Our Time*. New York: Beacon Press, 2001.
9 Robert Franklin Hoxie. *Scientific Management and Labour*. D. Appleton and Company, 1915.
10 Sarah Jaffe. *Work Won't Love You Back: How Devotion to Our Jobs Keeps Us Exploited, Exhausted and Alone*. C. Hurst & Co. Publishers, 2021.
11 Frederick Winslow Taylor. *Principles of Scientific Management*. London: Harper, 1911, p. 64.

12 John Philip Frey. 'Scientific Management and Labor', *American Federationist*. Vol. 23, 1916, p. 257.
13 Megan Carnegie. 'The Creepy Rise of Bossware.' *Wired*, 23 July 2023.
14 Andrew Fennell for Standout CV: 'Employee monitoring statistics.' 2023.
15 Brett Christophers. *Our Lives in Their Portfolios: Why Asset Managers Own the World*. Verso, 2023.
16 Mariana Mazzucato and Rosie Collington. *The Big Con*. Penguin Press, 2023, p. 157.
17 Ibid.
18 See also: Maurizio Zollo and Sidney G. Winter. 'From organisational routines to Dynamic Capabilities.' *The Insead Series*, 1999.
19 Camilla Heding Andersen, Lotte Maglehøj Hansen, Morten Willas Lund and Søren Obed Madsen. 'Gav det mening, skat?' *Samfundslederskab i Skandinavien*, 2018.
20 Lise Vesterlund, Linda Babcock, Brenda Peyser and Laurie Weingart. *The No Club: Putting a Stop to Women's Dead-End Work*. Simon & Schuster, 2022.
21 Fie Dandanell. 'Laver du flere opgaver, der er gode for firmaet, men dårlige for karrieren? Så tror jeg, at jeg kan gætte dit køn.' *Zetland*, 3 May 2022.
22 Anne Kirstine Cramon. 'Hvis du bager til dine kolleger, bliver du aldrig chef.' *Berlingske*, 9 September 2021.
23 Lise Vesterlund, Linda Babcock, Brenda Peyser and Laurie Weingart. *The No Club: Putting a Stop to Women's Dead-End Work*. Simon & Schuster, 2022, p. 73.
24 Judith Evans and Peter Smith. 'Bruce Flatt of Brookfield on owning the backbone of the global economy.' *Financial Times*, 22 September 2018.
25 Finn Amby. *Blinde og stærkt svagsynede i erhvervsuddannelserne: En kortlægning*. Ankerhus Gruppen Dansk and Blindesamfund, 2012.
26 Dorte Washuus. 'Gensyn med de blindes guldalder.' *Kristeligt Dagblad*, 12 October 2016.
27 Anette Claudi and Camilla Bresemann. '25årig med autisme er en succes i Elgiganten, og kollegerne elsker ham.' *TV2*, 21 December 2023.
28 Helen Schartz, Deborah Hendricks and Peter Blanck. 'Workplace accommodations: Evidence based outcomes', *Work*. Vol. 27, No. 4, 2006, pp. 345–54.

29 Teresa Almeida. 'Disability inclusion at work: the many not the few.' *LSE Business Review*, 31 March 2022: https://blogs.lse.ac.uk/businessreview/2022/03/31/disability-inclusion-at-work-the-many-not-the-few/
30 Torben Kajberg. 'Nye tal viser, at flere tusinde mennesker med handicap er klar til at arbejde.' Danske Handicaporganisationer, 9 November 2021.
31 John Zarocostas interview with Bob Ransom, senior specialist in vocational rehabilitation and employability with the International Labor Organization. 'Disabled still face hurdles in job market.' Washington Times, 5 December 2005.
32 'ENAR Shadow Report: Racism and Discrimination in Employment in Europe 2013–2017.' European Network Against Racism, 2018.
33 Mustafa F. Özbilgin and Natalia Slutskaya. 'Consequences of Neo-Liberal Politics on Equality and Diversity at Work in Britain: Is Resistance Futile?' in Jean-François Chanlat and Mustafa F. Özbilgin (eds). *Management and Diversity (International Perspectives on Equality, Diversity and Inclusion, Vol.4)*. Emerald Publishing Limited, 2017.
34 Freja Thorbech. 'Hvad gør KPI'erne ved dig? Ekspert advarer mod alvorlige bivirkninger.' *Finansforbundet*, 9 September 2024.
35 Karen Il Wol Knudsen. 'Analyse: 40 pct. af unge uden job og uddannelse har et handicap.' Danske Handicaporganisationer, 29 June 2022.
36 Andrew Natsios. 'The Clash of the Counter-Bureaucracy and Development.' *Hudson*, 1 July 2012, p. 1.
37 David Graeber. *Bullshit Jobs: A Theory*. Penguin UK, 2018.

Chapter 8: A Disservice to Public Services
1 Olivier Blanchard. 'Further Thoughts on DSGE Models: What we agree on and what we do not.' Peterson Institute of International Economics, 2016.
2 Servaas Storm. 'The Standard Economic Paradigm is Based on Bad Modeling.' Institute for New Economic Thinking, 2021.
3 Michaël Assous and Pedro Garcia Duarte. 'Challenging Lucas: From Overlapping Generations to Infinite-Lived Agent Models.' The Center for the History of Political Economy. Working Paper Series, 2017.

4   Robert Lucas. 'Economic Policy Evaluation: A Critique' in *The Phillips Curve and Labour Markets*, vol.1 of Carnegie-Rochester Conference Series on Public Policy, ed. Karl Brunner and Allan H. Melzer, Amsterdam: North-Holland Publishing Company, 1976.
5   Brandt Weathers. 'Lucas Critique After the Crisis: A Historicization and Review of one Theory's Eminence', *New School Economic Review*. Vol. 7, No. 1, 2015, p. 5.
6   Finn E. Kydland and Edward C. Prescott. 'Time to Build and Aggregate Fluctuations', *Econometrica*. Vol. 50, No. 6, 1982, pp. 1345–70.
7   Daniel Hirschman and Elizabeth Popp Berman. 'Do Economists Make Policies? On the Political Effects of Economics', *Socio-Economic Review*. Vol. 12, No. 4, 2014, pp. 779–811.
8   Lucas was quoted in: J. Cassidy. *How Markets Fail: the Logic of Economic Calamitie*. New York: Farrar, Straus and Giroux, 2009, p. 98.
9   Elizabeth Popp Berman. *Thinking Like an Economist: How Efficiency Replaced Equality in U.S. Public Policy*. Princeton University Press, 2022, p. 220.
10 Katherine Moos. 'The Transvaluation of the Theory of Economic Policy: The Lucas Critique Reconsidered.' The New School for Social Research working paper, 2016, p. 21.
11 Raphaël Fèvre. *A Political Economy of Power: Ordoliberalism in Context, 1932–1950*. Oxford University Press, 2021.
12 Interview with R. Lucas in Arjo Klamer. *Conversations with Economists*. Totowa, NJ: Rowman and Allanheld, 1983, p. 52.
13 Lars Andersen. 'Ændret syn på finanspolitikken?' *Samfundsøkonomen*, 1990.
14 The assumption that investments in public services do harm to the market is called 'crowding out'. Read more about the theory and its robustness here: Jamie Powell. 'The myth of crowding out.' *Financial Times*, 2 December 2019.
15 'De økonomiske vismænd: "Regnereglerne er ikke politiske, de er baserede på den tilgængelige evidens."' *Dagbladet Information*, 2 February, 2022.
16 Søren Hove Ravn. 'Finansministeriet skifter regnemaskinen ud.' *Altinget*, 31 January 2022.
17 Drucilla K. Barker. 'A feminist economist joins the conversation', *International Journal of Political Economy*. Vol. 50, No. 2, 2021, pp. 103–6.

18 David Colander, Richard P.F. Holt and J. Barkley Rosser, Jr. *The Changing Face of Economics: Conversations with Cutting Edge Economists*. Ann Arbor: University of Michigan Press, 2004, p. 293.
19 Joseph P. Newhouse and Insurance Experiment Group. *Free for all? Lessons from the Rand Health Insurance Experiment*. Harvard University Press, 1993.
20 Emil Hedman. '116 miljarder i över skott – ändå sparar kommuner på skolan.' *Vi Lärare*, 28 September 2023.
21 The point about unpredictability and separate parts comes from the discussion of complicated and complex systems. Read more here: Theodore Kinni. *The Critical Difference Between Complex and Complicated*. MITSloan Management Review, 2017. An additional nod to the economist Steve Keen, who says that not only care but the entire economy is a complicated system!
22 W. Brian Arthur. 'Economics in nouns and verbs', *Journal of Economic Behavior & Organization*. Vol. 205, 2023, pp. 638–47.
23 Joe Earle, Cahal Moran and Zach Ward-Perkins. *The econocracy: The perils of leaving economics to the experts*. Manchester University Press, 2016, p. 14.
24 Adam Tooze. *Statistics and the German State, 1900–1945*. Cambridge University Press, 2001.
25 Timothy Mitchell. 'Fixing the Economy', *Cultural Studies*. 12(1), 1998, pp. 82–101.
26 Diane Elson. 'Social Policy and Macroeconomic Performance: Integrating "the Economic" and "the Social"', in Thandika Mkandawire (ed.), *Social Policy in a Development Context*. Palgrave Macmillan, 2004, p. 67.
27 George A. Akerlof. 'Sins of Omission and the Practice of Economics', *Journal of Economic Literature*. Vol. 58, No. 2, 2020, pp. 405–18.
28 Paul Pfleiderer. 'Chameleons: The Misuse of Theoretical Models in Finance and Economics.' *Graduate School of Stanford Business: Working Paper No. 3020*, August 2018.
29 Villads Andersen. 'Kortere kandidater har udløst et talslagsmål blandt økonomer. Måske skal vi stoppe med at regne på alt?' Dagbladet Information, 11 March 2023.
30 'Baggrundsnotat om Reformkommissionens forslag om kortere kandidatuddannelser.' *Dansk Økonomi*. De Økonomiske Rad, 23 May 2022.

31 Edward E. Leamer. 'Tantalus on the Road to Asymptopia', *Journal of Economic Perspectives*. Vol. 24, No. 2, 2010, pp. 31–46.
32 John B. Shoven and John Whalley. 'Applied General Equilibrium Models of Taxation and International Trade: An Introduction and Survey', *Journal of Economic Literature*. Vol. 22, No. 3, 1984, pp. 1007–51.
33 Frank Van Lerven, Dominic Caddick and Sebastian Mang. 'Europe's Fiscal Framework – the People's View? How austerity made us poorer and less able to cope with crises.' New Economics Foundation, 4 November 2022, p. 4.
34 Frank Van Lerven, Dominic Caddick and Sebastian Mang. 'Europe's Fiscal Framework – the People's View? How austerity made us poorer and less able to cope with crises.' New Economics Foundation, 4 November 2022.
35 European Women's Lobby. 'The price of austerity – The impact on women's rights and gender equality in Europe.' 2012, p. 2.
36 Jo Michell. 'The Fable of the Ants, or Why the Representative Agent is No Such Thing.' criticalfinance.org, accessed 8 August 2024.
37 K.A. Horridge, R. Dew, A. Chatelin, A. Seal, L.M. Macias, G. Cioni, O. Kachmar, S. Wilkes. 'European Academy of Childhood Disability. Austerity and families with disabled children: a European survey', *Developmental Medicine and Child Neurology*. Vol. 61, No. 3, 2019, pp. 329–36.
38 All of the numbers related to health and austerity measures are from: D. Stuckler, A. Reeves, R. Loopstra, M. Karanikolos, M. McKee. 'Austerity and health: the impact in the UK and Europe', *European Journal of Public Health*. Vol. 27, No. 4, 2017, pp. 18–21.
39 Sarah Brown, Alexandros Kontonikas, Alberto Montagnoli, Mirko Moro, Luisanna Onnis. 'Life satisfaction and austerity: Expectations and the macroeconomy', *Journal of Behavioral and Experimental Economics*. Vol. 95, 2021.
40 Clare Bambra (ed.). *Health in Hard Times: Austerity and Health Inequalities*. 1st ed. Bristol University Press, 2019. The quote is from James Pearce's foreword.
41 Eurodad. 'End Austerity: A Global Report on Budget Cuts and Harmful Social Reforms in 2022–25', abstract. 28 September 2022
42 Derek Anderson et. al. 'Getting to Know GIMF: The Simulation Properties of the Global Integrated Monetary and Fiscal Model,' 22 February 2013.

43 Quote is from New Economics Foundation press release: 'Austerity policies have made European citizens €3000 a year worse-off', 4 November 2022. For accompanying graph, see Frank Van Lerven, Dominic Caddick and Sebastian Mang. 'Europe's Fiscal Framework – the People's View? How austerity made us poorer and less able to cope with crises.' New Economics Foundation, 4 November 2022, p. 12.
44 Niels Kærgård. 'Finansministeriet og makroøkonomiske regnemodeller: Et historisk rids.' *Samfundsøkonomen*, October 2020.
45 Oddný Helgadóttir. 'How to Make a Super-model: Professional Incentives and the Birth of Contemporary Macroeconomics', *Review of International Political Economy*. Vol. 30, 2023, pp. 252–80.
46 Anders Bæksgaard. 'Tidligere departementschef giver igen på kritik.' *Politiken*, 2 August 2018.
47 A summary of the fight over 'dilettantes' can be found in: Jo Michell. 'Dilettantes Shouldn't Get Excited.' criticalfinance.org, accessed 8 June 2024.
48 For some of the ways that feminist economics has challenged the existing paradigm, see: UN Women. 'Macroeconomic Policies for the Feminist Plan for Sustainability and Social Justice.' Expert Group Meeting Report, 2020.
49 Steve Keen. 'Predicting the "Global Financial Crisis": Post-Keynesian Macroeconomics', *Economic Record*. Vol. 89, No. 285, 2013, pp. 228–54.
50 Paul Romer. 'The Trouble with Macroeconomics.' Stern School of Business, New York University, 14 September 2016.
51 Paul Krugman. 'The State of Macro Is Sad (Wonkish).' *New York Times*, 12 August 2016.
52 Paul Krugman, 'Lionel Robbins Lecture.' Lecture, London School of Economics, 10 June 2009.
53 Joseph E. Stiglitz. 'Where modern macroeconomics went wrong', *Oxford Review of Economic Policy*. Vol. 34, No. 1–2, Spring–Summer 2018, pp. 70–106.
54 Jeremy B. Rudd. *A Practical Guide to Macro Economics*. Cambridge University Press, 2024, p. 186.
55 There is incredible work being done to model care in macroeconomics. You can find more of this work here: 'Feminist Perspectives on Care and Macroeconomic Modelling: Introduction to the Special Issue', *Feminist Economics*. Vol. 28, 2022.

56 Alfred Marshall. *Principles of Economics*. 1920. https://www.marxists.org/reference/subject/economics/marshall/bk1ch02.htm
57 Thomas Franks. 'David Graeber: "Spotlight on the financial sector did make apparent just how bizarrely skewed our economy is in terms of who gets rewarded."' Salon.com, 1 June 2014.

Chapter 9: Beating Hearts in a Broken System
1 'Kvinder koster samfundet 12 millioner kroner gennem livet.' *Nettavisen*, 30 March 2022.
2 International Labour Organization (ILO). *Care Work and Care Jobs for the Future of Decent Work*. Geneva: ILO, 2018, p. 165.
3 'The gender pay gap in the health and care sector: a global analysis in the time of COVID-19.' Geneva: World Health Organization and the International Labour Organization, 2022, p. 4.
4 Julian Jessop. 'Our public services are hamstrung by low productivity.' *Critic*, 23 November 2023.
5 International Labour Organization (ILO). *Care Work and Care Jobs for the Future of Decent Work*. Geneva: ILO, 2018, p. 172.
6 Paula England. 'Emerging theories of care work', *Annual Review of Sociology*. Vol. 31, 2005, p. 390.
7 Birthe Larsen. 'Løngabet for sygeplejersker er reelt.' *Politiken*, 20 June 2021.
8 Nancy Fraser. 'Contradictions of capital and care.' *New Left Review*, July/August 2016.
9 WHO. 'Topics – Health Workforce.' https://www.who.int/health-topics/health-workforce#tab=tab_1, accessed 8 September 2024.
10 European center for development of vocational training. 'Handling change with care – Skills for the EU care sector.' 2023, p. 4.
11 'Ready for the Next Crisis? Investing in Health System Resilience.' OECD Health Policy Studies, OECD Publishing, Paris, 2023.
12 Richard Adams. 'Record numbers of teachers in England quitting profession, figures show.' *Guardian*, 8 June 2023.
13 Finansministeriet. 'Sygehusene fritages for produktivitetskrav i 2018'. *Regeringen*, 4 October 2017.
14 Susanne Ekman. 'Offentlig ledelse som gearing og gældsspekulation: Hvordan besparelser og effektiviseringskrav lærer den offentlige sektor at love mere end den kan holde' in Louise Li

Langergaard and Katia Dupret. *Social Bæredygtighed: Begreb, felt og kritik*. Frydenlund Academic, 2020.
15. A. Atkinson. 'Final Report, Measurement of Government Output and Productivity for the National Accounts.' 31 January 2005, p. 186.
16. World Bank Group. 'Public-Sector Productivity (Part 1) Why is it important and how can we measure it?', February 2021, p. 8. https://documents1.worldbank.org/curated/en/913321612847439794/pdf/Public-Sector-Productivity-Part-One-Why-Is-It-Important-and-How-Can-We-Measure-It.pdf
17. Produktivitetskommissionen. *Måling af produktivitet i den offentlige sektor – metodemæssige udfordringer*. Produktivitetskommissionen, 2013.
18. OECD. 'Compendium of Productivity Indicators.' 2024, p. 49.
19. Ravi Somani. 'How can we measure productivity in the public sector?' World Bank Blogs. 4 March 2021. See also World Bank Group. 'Public-Sector Productivity (Part 1) Why is it important and how can we measure it?' 2021, p. 20.
20. A. Atkinson. 'Final Report, Measurement of Government Output and Productivity for the National Accounts.' 31 January 2005, p. 5
21. Perverse consequences comes from: Richard Boyle, 'Public sector productivity measurement: an impossible task?' in *Perspectives on Irish Productivity*. DETE, 2007, p. 108.
22. Sandra Dawson and Charlotte Dargie. 'New Public Management: A discussion with special reference to UK health' in Kathleen McLaughlin, Ewan Ferlie and Stephen Osborne. *New Public Management*. Routledge, 2001.
23. John Gledhill. 'Neoliberalism' in David Nugent and Joan Vincent. *A Companion to the Anthropology of Politics*. John Wiley & Sons, 2004, p. 341.
24. Michael Power. *The Audit Society*. Oxford: Oxford University Press, 1997.
25. OECD. 'Health at a glance – 2023 edition.' https://www.oecd.org/en/publications/2023/11/health-at-a-glance-2023_e04f8239.html
26. Paula McFadden. 'Measuring burnout among UK social workers – A Community Care study.' 2015, p. 29. https://www.qub.ac.uk/sites/media/Media,514081,en.pdf
27. Ibid.
28. Emilie Lichtenberg. 'Flere oplever stress – især blandt offentligt ansatte [Analyse].' Arbejderbevægelsens Erhvervsråd, 9 August 2018.

29 Rosa Suñer-Soler, Armand Grau-Martín, Daniel Flichtentrei, Maria Prats, Florencia Braga, Silvia Font-Mayolas, Mª Eugenia Gras. 'The consequences of burnout syndrome among healthcare professionals in Spain and Spanish speaking Latin American countries', *Burnout Research*. Vol. 1, No. 2, 2014, pp. 82–9.
30 Susanne Ekman. 'Offentlig ledelse som gearing og gældsspekulation: Hvordan besparelser og effektiviseringskrav lærer den offentlige sektor at love mere end den kan holde' in Louise Li Langergaard and Katia Dupret. *Social bæredygtighed: Begreb, felt og kritik*. Frydenlund Academic, 2020, pp. 103–32.
31 Anna Fazackerly. 'Nurseries in England Say New Rules Have Reduced Care to "Crowd Control."' *Guardian*, 14 September 2024. https://www.theguardian.com/education/2024/sep/14/nurseries-in-england-say-new-rules-have-reduced-care-to-crowd-control
32 'Psykiatrien er presset – patienter får ikke den behandling de har behov for.' Dansk Psykolog Forening, 30 April 2022.
33 Ditte Ravn Jakobsen. "Man mister mening i sit arbejde" Efter 16 år kan Maria næsten ikke kende sit fag mere.' *Politiken*, 30 April 2022.
34 Karen Ravn. 'Vismand: Kvaliteten af skolen bør indgå i nationalregnskabet.' *Folkeskolen*, 6 March 2019.
35 Line Vaaben. 'Jens kan ikke bevæge sig fra halsen og ned. Kommunen vil have taget tid på, hvor længe hans kone er om at pudse hans næse.' *Politiken*, 17 September 2023.
36 'Kapitel IV: Tidlig indsats.' *Dansk Økonomi, Forår 2021*. De Økonomiske Råd, 2021.
37 Steven Van de Walle. 'NPM: Restoring the public trust through creating distrust?' in *The Ashgate Research Companion to New Public Management*. Farnham: Ashgate, 2016, pp. 309–20.
38 Marie Hein Plum. 'Socialrådgivere: Vi bruger 82 procent af arbejdstiden på papirarbejde.' Avisen.dk, 23 September 2016.
39 Helle Øbo. *Man møder et menneske*. Akademisk Forlag, 2023, p. 86.
40 David Brindle. 'Buurtzorg: the Dutch model of neighbourhood care that is going global.' *Guardian*, 9 May 2017.
41 KPMG International. 'Value Walks: Successful habits for improving workforce motivation and productivity in healthcare.' KPMG, 2016.
42 R. Baeten, S. Spasova, B. Vanhercke and S. Coster. 'Inequalities in access to healthcare. A study of national policies.' European

Social Policy Network (ESPN), Brussels: European Commission, 2018, p. 7.
43 Dorte Quist. 'Ulighed følger dig I graven: De fattigste mænd dør 10 år før de rigeste.' *Faglige Seniorer*, 19 February 2021.
44 *Jo mere udsat – jo mere syg. Om socialt udsatte danskeres sundhed og sygdom.* Rådet for Socialt Udsatte, 2014.
45 'Mödradödlighet drabbar olika i Sverige.' Uppsala Universitet, 17 March 2014.
46 Andreas Rudkjøbing et al. '12 aktører med opråb til politikerne: Afskaf diskriminerende tolkegebyr.' *Altinget*, 23 September 2019.

Conclusion

1 Evelyne Hübscher, Thomas Sattler and Markus Wagner. 'Does Austerity Cause Polarization?', *British Journal of Political Science*. Vol. 53, No. 4, 2023, pp. 1170–88.
2 Sheila Rowbotham. *Women's Consciousness, Men's World*. Pelican, 1973, p. 30.

ILLUSTRATION CREDITS

p. 15 Graphs showing child penalties across countries. Adapted from paper by Henrik Kleven, Camille Landais, Johanna Posch, Andreas Steinhauer and Josef Zweimüller: 'Child Penalties across Countries: Evidence and Explanations', *AEA Papers and Proceedings*, Vol. 109, May 2019, pp. 122–6. With permission from the authors.

p. 31 Images from *Le Roman de la Rose* © Bibliothèque nationale de France.

p. 33 Title page of *A Candle in the Dark*, courtesy of the Wellcome Collection. In the public domain, under Attribution 4.0 International (CC BY 4.0) licence.

p. 40 Illustration of the pain pathway in René Descartes' *Traite de l'homme* (Treatise of Man), 1664. Sourced from Wikimedia Commons, in the public domain.

p. 42 Illustrated title page of 'The Parliament of Women', from the British Library archive © British Library/ Bridgeman.

p. 74 Pin maker's factory, as depicted in Diderot's *Encyclopédie*, courtesy of The Picture Art Collection / Alamy Stock Photo.

p. 134 Graph showing Danish child penalty, adapted from paper by Henrik Kleven, Camille Landais and Jakob Egholt Søgaard: 'Children and Gender Inequality: Evidence from Denmark', *American Economic Journal: Applied Economic*, Vol. 11, no. 4, October 2019, pp. 181–209. With permission from the authors.

p. 186 *Ms.* magazine cover, Spring 1972 issue. Liberty Media for Women, LLC. Released to Wikimedia Commons under the Creative Commons Attribution-Share Alike 4.0 International license housewife.

p. 206 Screenshot from YouTube video 'NeuroSpot Baristaeye Staff Control and Customer Monitoring Video Analytics Module', uploaded in May 2023. Reproduced courtesy of NeuroSpot.

p. 224 Emma in hospital © Steve McFarland.

INDEX

Aboriginal peoples, Jevons on 109–10, 135
abortion, right to access 182
Ackerman, Frank 114
Adam Smith Institute 82–3, 85
AI (artificial intelligence) for employee surveillance 205, *206*
Akerlof, George 242
Andersen, Lars 231
Ariadad, Samira 89
Arrow, Kenneth 105–6, 235
Arruzza, Cinzia 175
Arthur, William Brian 239
Astell, Mary 54–5
austerity policies 131–2, 244–8

bank holidays 122–3
bankers 101, 104
Barbie (Gertwig movie) 166–7, 174
Barker, Drucilla 235
Beckles-Raymond, Gabriella 179
benefits, *see* social welfare
Benería, Lourdes 112
Benhabib, Seyla 63–4, 83, 161
Berlin, Isaiah 62–3
Beveridge, William 123–4
Bhattacharya, Tithi 136, 175
Bieber, Justin 31
birth rates, economic concerns 154–6

Bispebjerg Hospital, Copenhagen 3, 5, 223, *224*, 234, 244
Bjørnskov, Christian 139
Black women 166, 171–3, 175–9, 181–4
Blok, Jos de 270–1
bodily needs and functions:
  economic actors assumed to lack, see *Homo economicus* (rational economic actor)
  fear and shame arising from 45–6, 54–5, 59–60, 63–5, 89, 282
  historical distrust of 20, 28–9, 39–40, *40*, 45, 53–4
  marginalist economists' disregard for 98–9
  procreation, *see* procreation
  sex without procreation aim 35, 36, 37–8
  see also emotions and mental health; nature
Bodin, Jean 34–8
Borchorst, Anette 184–5
Boyle, Richard 260
Braverman, Suella 112
breastfeeding 135, 153
Brøchner Madsen, Jakob 115–16
Brontë, Charlotte 119
Brown, Wendy 199
Burke, Edmund 93

Cagatay, Nilufer 241

Candle in the Dark, A (Ady) 33
care work:
  feminist perspectives on, *see* feminist perspectives on care work
  gender roles, culturally determined 12–14, 112–13, 150–4, 185–9, 190–1
  history of ideas on, *see* Enlightenment era; marginalism; pre-Enlightenment era
  as 'investment' in oneself 199–200
  need for
    fear and shame arising from 45–6, 54–5, 59–60, 63–5, 89, 282
    illusory freedom from 66–7, 161–3, 193
  professional
    health and social care workers, *see* health and social care sector
    maids and nannies 57, 58–9, 104, 126, 172–3, 175–7, 182–4
  public spending on, *see* public spending on care
  skills required for 188–9
  unpaid, *see* childcare; housework
  value of, *see* value of care work
  in workplaces ('non-promotable tasks' idea) 209–11, 214, 218–19
Carter, Zachary 170
Chapman, Edmund 41, 43
child bearing, *see* procreation
childcare:
  breastfeeding 135, 153
  child penalty data 15, 16, 133–4, 143, 153
  Collier's poem on 47–8
  family and community structures for 12–14, 152–3, 179
  fathers' sense of exclusion from 179–80, 192
  men's 'weaponised incompetence' at 185, 187–9
  mothers, disparagement of 64–5
  nannies 104, 172–3
  part time work by parents 142–3, 144–5, 161–2
  'screen rearing' 192–3
  sick or disabled children 146–50, 189–90, 246–7
  by single mothers 245
  state intervention affecting 181–2
  stress and depression associated with 134, 164–5
  by teachers and nursery staff 237, 257, 266
  value of, *see* value of care work
  see also housework; procreation
Christensen, Inger 275
Christophers, Brett 205, 206–7
Clark, John Bates 197
classical economics, *see* Smith, Adam
Cody, Lisa Forman 43, 44
Collier, Mary 47–8

Collington, Rosie 207–8
colonialism (practice and theory) 18–19, 110, 128–9, 135, 181–4, 282
communism, US policies opposing (1940s–50s) 167–8, 169–70, 249–50
contract theory (Locke) 56
Cooley, Charles Horton 60
Cooper, Frederick 128–9
cost-benefit analysis:
  generally 124–5, 136
  for public services delivery 260–4, 268–71
  in workplaces, see human resources management
COVID-19 pandemic 147–8
Coyle, Diane 7–8, 130

Dalgaard, Carl-Johan 122
Dalla Costa, Mariarosa 150–1, 180
Dargie, Charlotte 261
Davis, Angela 176, 178, 183
Dawson, Sandra 261
De Corpore (Hobbes) 52
De la démonomanie des sorciers (Bodin) 35
Deane, Phyllis 128, 129
Debreu, Gérard 105–6
democracy:
  established economics, democratic deficit 93, 279–81
  Locke on 55–6, 62, 65
  see also freedom; human rights
Denmark:
  demographic trends 154–5, 272

disabled people's workforce participation 211–14, 216
DSGE macroeconomic model 226, 234
economic advice to Government 4–5, 10, 116, 242–3
environmental policies 137, 138–9
GDP (gross domestic product) 22–3, 131–2
Great Prayer Day abolition 122–3
mental health crisis in 198
migrants, policies aimed at 173, 181–2, 183–4
paternity leave in 192
sick leave data 145–6, 147
tax authority, mass redundancies at 208–9
unpaid hours spent on care work (by gender) 14, 16, 133, 134, 189
women's salaries 15, 16, 113, 133–4
women's workforce participation 143, 144–5, 184–5
Descartes, René 39–40, 40
diamonds 97, 98, 100
Dijksterhuis, Eduard Jan 46
disabled people:
  children, care for 189–90, 246–7
  workforce participation 211–14, 216
domestic labour, see childcare; housework
Douglas, Janet 76–7, 80
Douglas, Margaret 76–7, 80–1, 172, 173
drugs, as part of GDP 130

DSGE (dynamic stochastic general equilibrium) models, *see* macroeconomic models

ecofeminism 136, 241
economics, *see* established economics; feminist economics; marginalism
'economy' concept 240–1
education services 237, 242–3, 257, 266
Ekman, Susanne 258, 266
elderly people, care for 65, 236, 245, 247, 270–1
Elizabeth II 116
Elson, Diane 241
emotions and mental health:
 care work, stress associated with 134, 164–5, 265–7
 historical distrust of emotions 20, 28–32, 41–5
 madwoman archetype 71, 86–7, 89
 of men 151, 180, 194
 mental health crisis, Western states 197–8, 208–9, 246–7
 psychological care services 238, 267
 Smith's understanding of 80–1, 84–5
 see also bodily needs and functions
employee surveillance technology 205, *206*; *see also* human resources management
enclosure of common land (18th century England) 72
England, *see* United Kingdom

England, Paula 174
Enlightenment era:
 care work, disregard for 53–5, 56–9, 60–2, 63–4, 66–7, 75, 79–81, 88
 distrust of women and emotions 41–5
 economic and political theories
  of Hobbes 39, 51–5, 57, 58, 65, 87–8, 98
  of Locke, *see* Locke, John
  of Smith, *see* Smith, Adam
 mechanical view of nature and the body 38–40, *40*, 45–6, 53–4
 rationality value 20, 27–8, 32–4, 84–5, 87–8
 see also pre-Enlightenment era
enslaved women 183
environmental harm 127, 136–40, 141–2, 241
equilibrium theories:
 general equilibrium theory 105–6, 110–11, 114–15
 macroeconomic models based on, *see* macroeconomic models
 of marginalism 94–5, 99–101
 of Samuelson 169–70
Esscher, Annika 273
established economics:
 assumptions and predictions 12–14, 107–9, 114–16, 149–50, 191
 rational economic actors, see *Homo economicus* (rational economic actor)
 care work unappreciated by, *see* value of care work

cost-benefit analysis 124–5, 136
  for public service delivery 260–4, 268–71
  in workplaces, *see* human resources management
democratic deficit 93, 279–81
free market logic 81–4, 170, 230–1, 255–6
  human capital theory 199–200, 207–9
  market failure idea 113–14, 137–8
GDP metric, *see* GDP (gross domestic product)
as language of power 6–10, 18–19, 127, 149, 168–71, 240–1
macroeconomic models, *see* macroeconomic models
neutrality façade 9, 12–13, 85–6, 111–12, 139–40, 171, 228–30
origins, *see* Enlightenment era; marginalism
see also feminist economics
European Union 7, 18, 130, 131–2, 244

factory work 72–4, 74, 202–3, 267
fathers 15, 113, 149–50, 153, 161–3, 179–80, 192; *see also* childcare
Federici, Silvia 30, 36, 150–1
Fee, Liz 41
Feminine Mystique, The (Friedan) 163–7

feminist economics:
  care work appreciated by 21–2, 48, 173–5, 177–9, 280, 283–4
  criticisms of 121–3, 250, 281–2
  ecologically informed 136, 241
  key concepts 11–12, 19, 23–4
  relational welfare idea 269–71
  Wages for Housework movement 150–4, 175, 180
  see also established economics
feminist perspectives on care work:
  Black/marginalised women's experiences, disregard for 166, 171–3, 175–9, 181–4
  multitasking woman archetype 185, *186*, 190–1
  as oppression 21, 144, 164–7, 176–7
  value appreciated 21–2, 48, 173–5, 177–9, 280, 283–4
  women's paid work as freedom 144, 163–4, 165, 176–7, 179–81
Ferguson, Susan 164
fertility rates, economic concerns 154–6
financial crisis (2007–08) 115–16, 131, 141–2, 244, 250–1
Finland, estimated value of care work in 140
Flatt, Bruce 211
Folbre, Nancy 58, 111
forced sterilisation policies 182
Fourcade, Marion 9–10

Franczak, Michael 18
Fraser, Nancy 173–4, 175, 256
freedom:
   from care/care-giving needs 66–7, 161–3, 193
   care work viewed as oppression 21, 144, 164–7, 176–7
   Enlightenment ideas on 55–7, 58–9, 60–1, 62–6, 87–8
   women's paid work viewed as 144, 163–4, 165, 176–7, 179–81
   see also democracy; human rights
Friedan, Betty 163–7, 172, 174, 175, 176–7, 178
friendship 198, 199

Galileo Galilei 52
Galtier, Brigitte 150–1
GDP (gross domestic product):
   adoption of 21, 125
   borrowing and spending powers determined by 129–32
   care work, disregard for 126–7, 129, 132–6, 139–40, 157
   cross-country GDP comparisons 22–3
   environmental harm, disregard for 127, 136–42, 241
   geopolitical implications 127–9
   mental health crisis unlinked to 197–8
   prices based on 125–8

gender-based violence and discrimination 23, 59–60, 113–14, 165, 173, 177–9
gender roles, culturally determined 12–14, 112–13, 150–4, 185–9, 190–1
general equilibrium theory 105–6, 110–11, 114–15
Germany, child penalty data 153
'ghetto law' (Denmark) 181
Gies, Frances 30
Gies, Joseph 30
Gledhill, Jonathan 261–2
global financial crisis (2007–08) 115–16, 131, 141–2, 244, 250–1
Goodhart's law 218
Graeber, David 85, 252
Grande, Ariana 91
Gray, John 30–1
Greece, austerity policies in 246
gross domestic product, *see* GDP (gross domestic product)

health and social care sector:
   hospitals, care work in 223, 225, 235–6
   low wages and disparagement of workers 5, 64–5, 101–3, 126–7, 255–7, 268–9
   midwives (female), historical distrust of 35, 41–2, 44
   part time work in 143
   public spending on, *see* public spending on care
   sick leave, public sector workers 145–50
   stress and burnout in 265–7

underprivileged citizens' access barriers 271–3
unpaid workers as 'buffer' for 236, 245–6
workers by gender 16, 147–8
Hedva, Johanna 221
Heinsohn, Gunnar 37
Helgadóttir, Oddný 249
Hirschman, Daniel 229
historical perspectives, *see* Enlightenment era; pre-Enlightenment era
Hobbes, Thomas 39, 51–5, 57, 58, 65, 87–8, 98
Hochschild, Arlie Russell 185
holidays, national 122–3
homelessness 112
Homo economicus (rational economic actor):
  afterlife of idea 81–4, 85–6, 88, 95, 112–13
  illusory independence of 161–3
  marginalists' rational consumer 108–11, 235, 236–7
  'representative agent' of DSGE models 227, 228–9, 232, 272
  Smith on self-interest of 76–9, 84–5, 87–8
hooks, bell 163, 171–2, 173
hospitals, *see* health and social care sector
housework:
  Collier's poem on 47–8
  hours spent on (by gender) 14, 16, 133, 134, 189
  labour-saving devices for 106, 107
  servants performing 57, 58–9, 104, 126, 172–3, 175–7, 182–4
  value of, *see* value of care work
  see also childcare
human resources management:
  diverse workforces, disincentives for 211–17
  human capital theory 199–200, 207–9
  mental health crisis arising from 197–8, 208–9
  'non-promotable tasks' idea 209–11, 214, 218–19
  scientific approach (Taylorism) 200–5, *206*
human rights:
  abortion, right to access 182
  clean environment right proposal 139
  Enlightenment ideas on 62–3, 66–7
  limitations of 279–80
  marginalist economists' disregard for 98–9
  see also democracy; freedom

Indigenous populations 109–10, 135, 181–2
International Labour Organization 256
International Monetary Fund 18, 226, 233, 244, 248
'invisible hand' metaphor (Smith) 77–9, 82, 84, 85
Italy, demographic trends 156, 247

James, Selma 150–1, 180
Jessop, Julian 255–6
Jevons, William Stanley 94, 95, 99, 108, 109–10, 135, 262
Al-Jizani, Lara Saleem Yousif 273
Johnson, Boris 185

Kærgård, Niels 248–9
Keynes, John Maynard 123–4, 125, 169, 170, 228
King, Martin Luther 168
King, Mervyn 259–60
Knight, Frank 99
Koch brothers (Charles and David) 170, 171, 249–50
Kramer, Heinrich 29–30
Krugman, Paul 6–7, 85–6, 250–1
Kuznets, Simon 125, 127–8

Lapeyre, Louis 44
Larsen, Birthe 256
Lassen, Anne Sophie 116–17
Lazear, Edward 19
Le Roman de la Rose 31
Leake, John 44
Leamer, Edward 243
Lerner, Gerda 165–6, 167, 171
Lerner, Max 72–3
Leviathan (Hobbes) 39, 51–2, 53–5
Liu, Glory M. 84
Locke, John:
  on care work 56–7, 60–2, 75, 79
  on democracy and freedom 55–7, 58–9, 60–1, 65–6, 82, 87–8
  on 'waste' land 135

loneliness epidemic in Western states 198
Loos, Cornelius 32
Lorde, Audre 159
Louis, Édouard 25
Lucas, Robert 228, 229, 230–1, 251
Lüneborg, Poul 212–13
luxury good purchases 106–7

macroeconomic models:
  adoption of 227–30
  anti-state nihilism of 230–2
  care work, disregard for 232–9, 241, 245–6
  price and value indistinguishable in 232–4, 235–9, 242–4
  'representative agent' of 227, 228–9, 232, 272
  widespread use and traction 226, 248–52
  see also equilibrium theories
Mad Men (television series) 31–2
madwoman archetype 71, 86–7, 89
maids and nannies 57, 58–9, 104, 126, 172–3, 175–7, 182–4
Malleus Maleficarum (Kramer) 29–30
Mankiw, Gregory 6–7
Marçal, Katrine 76
marginalism:
  afterlife, *see* established economics
  consumer demand ideas 97–100, 107–11, 114–15
  equilibrium theory 94–5, 99–101

natural science basis claim 93–6, 99–101, 197
post-Second World War rejection of 123–4
price theory 17, 21, 96–8, 101–2, 121–3
utopian socialists' critique of 102–3
market failure idea 113–14, 137–8
Marshall, Alfred 96, 252
Martinez, Elizabeth 178
mathematics, *see* science and mathematics
Mather, Cotton 45
Mazzucato, Mariana 97, 127, 207–8
McKinsey (management consultancy firm) 142, 143
measurable workplaces:
  performance indicators 217–18
  workforces, *see* human resources management
men (cisgender):
  distrust of women encouraged 29–34
  emotions and mental health 151, 180, 194
  fathers 15, 113, 149–50, 153, 161–3, 179–80, 192
  male midwives of Enlightenment era 41, 43–4
  as rational economic actors, *see* Homo economicus (rational economic actor)
  unpaid hours spent on care work 14, 16, 133, 134, 189
  'weaponised incompetence' portrayals 185, 187–9
  women urged to emulate 21, 165, 179–80, 185, 193–4
  workforce participation 142–3, 145, 161–2
Menger, Carl 94, 95, 99
mental health, *see* emotions and mental health
mercantilism, link to witch hunts 34–8
#MeToo movement 173
Middle Ages, *see* pre-Enlightenment era
middle managers 216
midwives (female), historical distrust of 35, 41, 43–4
Mies, Maria 32
migrant workers 173, 181–4, 214–15
Milanović, Branko 100
Mitchell, Timothy 240
Moos, Katherine 230–1
mothers, *see* childcare; procreation
Msimang, Sisonke 61–2
multitasking woman archetype 185, *186*, 190–1
mushrooms, as social beings 67, 141

nannies and maids 57, 58–9, 104, 126, 172–3, 175–7, 182–4
narcotics, as part of GDP 130
national holidays 122–3
Natsios, Andrew 217–18
nature:
  Enlightenment views on 38–9, 45–6, 53–4, 135
  environmental harm 127, 136–40, 141–2, 241

marginalism, natural science claim 93–6, 99–101, 197
see also bodily needs and functions
needle manufacture 73–4, 74
Nelson, Julie 38–9, 112
neoclassical economics, see marginalism
neutrality façade of established economics 9, 12–13, 85–6, 111–12, 139–40, 171, 228–30
New Deal economic policies (US, 1930s) 168–9
New Economics Foundation 104, 244–5, 248
New Public Management (NPM) 260–4, 268–9, 270
Nihell, Elizabeth 43–4
Nobel Memorial Prize in Economic Sciences 251
non-governmental organisations (NGOs) 217–18
'non-promotable tasks' idea 209–11, 214, 218–19
Nordhaus, William 108–9
NPM (New Public Management) 260–4, 268–9, 270
nuclear families 12–14, 152–3, 191–2
Nyrop, Martin 223

Øbo, Helle 269–70
O'Brien, Mark 253
OECD (Organisation for Economic Co-operation and Development) 127, 259, 265
Overbeek, Johannes 37
Özbilgin, Mustafa F. 215

parenting, see childcare

Parliament of Women (satirical pamphlet, 1646) 41, 42
part time work 142–3, 144–5, 161–2
paternity leave 179–80, 192
peasant rebellions 20, 39
penis trees 30, 31
performance indicators, workplace 217–18
personnel management, see human resources management
Pigou, Arthur Cecil 125
Polanyi, Karl 199–200
pollution 127, 136–40, 141–2, 241
Popp Berman, Elizabeth 229
Poulain de la Barre, François 58
Power, Michael 262
pre-Enlightenment era:
distrust of women in 20, 28–34, 35–7
mercantilism, link to witch hunts 34–8
see also Enlightenment era
price:
GDP (gross domestic product) and 125–8
price theory of marginalism 17, 21, 96–8, 101–2, 121–3
value distinguished from 17–18, 137–42, 232–4, 235–9, 242–4, 258–9, 278–9
private equity firms 205, 206–7, 211
procreation:
abortion, right to access 182
childless women, public discourse on 13, 156–7

fertility rates, economic
    concerns 154–6
forced sterilisation policies
    182
maternal deaths 153, 273
mercantilism on 34–8
midwives (female), historical
    distrust of 35, 41–2, 44
see also bodily needs and
    functions; childcare
public spending on care:
  care debt from underfunding
      265–7
  disparaged 103–4, 230–4
  fiscal rules restricting 131–2,
      244–8
  political division from
      underfunding 280–1
  productivity and efficiency
      aims linked to 257–9,
      260–4, 268–71
  'reverse Robin Hood' effect
      from underfunding 271–3
  unpaid workers 'buffering'
      effects of cuts 236, 245–6
  value of care work, unrelated
      to, see value of care work

quantifiable workplaces:
  performance indicators
      217–18
  workforces, see human
      resources management

rational economic actors, see
    Homo economicus (rational
    economic actor)
rationality value of
  Enlightenment era 20, 27–8,
      32–4, 84–5, 87–8

Red Scare (US anti-communism
    policies, 1940s–50s) 167–8,
    169–70, 249–50
relational welfare approach
    269–71
reproduction, see care work;
    procreation
respect, human need for 60, 89
rights, see human rights
Robinson, Joan 8, 78
Romer, Paul 250
Ronchi, Maddalena 113
Roosevelt, Franklin D. 168–9
Rothschild, Emma 78
Rowbotham, Sheila 282
Rowntree, Seebohm 123–4
Rudd, Jeremy B. 251

Samuelson, Paul 8, 108–9, 124,
    169–70, 171
sanitation workers 104
Schlefer, Jonathan 114
science and mathematics:
  in Enlightenment era 27, 32,
      38–9, 42, 44–5, 51–2
  established economics
      aspiring to 6–9, 17–19,
      85–6, 111–12, 202, 228–30,
      251
  natural science claim of
      marginalism 93–6, 99–101,
      197
  scientific management
      (Taylorism) 200–5, *206*
'screen rearing' of children
    192–3
Sear, Rebecca 152–3
Secher, Maria Holmgaard 267
Second World War, economics
    in 124–5

secretary archetype 187
sedative prescriptions 164–5
servants, domestic 57, 58–9, 104, 126, 172–3, 175–7, 182–4
sex without procreation aim 35, 36, 37–8
sex work, as part of GDP 130
sexual violence and discrimination 23, 59–60, 113–14, 165, 173, 177–9
Shah, Sumitra 75
sick leave, public sector workers 145–50
Simone, Nina 49
Skidelsky, Robert 109
slaves, female 183
Slutskaya, Natalia 215
Smith, Adam:
  'invisible hand' metaphor 77–9, 82, 84, 85
  on mechanised efficiency 72–4
  on self-interest of *Homo economicus* 76–9, 84–5, 87–8
  on supply and demand 97
  on women's economic and care roles 75, 79–81
Smith, Nina 113
social care sector, *see* health and social care sector
social contract theory (Locke) 56
social value theory 104
social welfare:
Danish official statistics 4–5
New Deal economic policies (US, 1930s) 168–9
post-Second World War economists on 123–4
public spending on, *see* public spending on care
Scandinavian model 278
socialism, utopian 102–3
socially marginalised women 166, 171–3, 175–9, 181–4
Socrates 28–9, 40
Solnit, Rebecca 149
Sørensen, Peter Birch 137
Spears, Britney 20, 71, 86–7, 89
Steiger, Otto 37
Stiglitz, Joseph 251
Stone, Richard 129
Storm, Servaas 226
Switzerland, child penalty data 15

Táíwò, Olúfẹ́mi O. 18
Tarshis, Lorie 169, 170, 171
Taylor, Frederick Winslow (and Taylorism) 200–5, *206*
teachers 237, 257, 266
Thatcher, Margaret 103
Theory of Moral Sentiments, The (Smith) 79, 81, 84
think tanks 82
Thompson, William 102–3
time and motion studies 200–5, *206*
Tooze, Adam 240
Traité de l'Homme (Descartes) 40
Trucost (environmental consultancy firm) 136–7
Trump, Donald 185, 250
Two Treatises of Government (Locke) 55–7

Ukraine war (2022–) 132
ulcerative colitis 3, 60, 225

United Kingdom:
  austerity policies, impact in 247
  Black women's experiences in 179
  care work, estimated value in 140, 258
  care worker shortages in 257
  child penalty data 15
  GDP (gross domestic product) 23, 130
  gender politics in 4
  loneliness epidemic in 198
  paternity leave in 192
  sick leave data 146–7
  women's workforce participation 142, 145
United Nations 18, 125
United States:
  Black women's experiences in 177, 178
  child penalty data 15
  GDP (gross domestic product) 23
  gender politics in 13
  life expectancy in 141–2
  loneliness epidemic in 198
  maternal deaths data 153
  New Deal economic policies (1930s) 168–9
  paternity leave in 192
  Red Scare (anti-communism policies, 1940s-50s) 167–8, 169–70, 249–50
  sedative prescriptions for mothers 164–5
  sick leave data 147
unpaid care work, *see* childcare; housework

utopian socialism 102–3
Valium prescriptions 164–5
value of care work:
  central paradox of 277–8
  disparaged 64–5, 103–4, 111–13, 126–7, 230–4, 255–7, 268–9
  feminist appreciation 21–2, 48, 173–5, 177–9, 280, 283–4
  GDP calculations disregarding 126–7, 129, 132–6, 139–40, 157
  macroeconomic models disregarding 232–9, 241, 245–6
  methods of determining 104, 116–17, 126, 140, 259–60
  relational welfare approach 269–71
  value and price distinction 17–18, 137–42, 232–4, 235–9, 242–4, 258–9, 278–9
  Wages for Housework movement 150–4, 175, 180
Vance, JD 13
Vesterlund, Lise 209–10
Vilkår, Lige 189

Wages for Housework movement 150–4, 175, 180
van de Walle, Steven 268
Walras, Léon 94, 95, 99, 103, 108
Ware, Bronnie 194
Waring, Marilyn 132–3
Wasner, Evan 114
Wealth of Nations, The (Smith), *see* Smith, Adam
Weber, Isabella 114

welfare state, *see* social welfare
Wheeler, Anna 102–3
witch hunts and trials 29–30, 32, *33*, 34–7
Wittman, Carl 162
Woman's Labour, The (Collier) 47–8
women (cisgender):
   austerity policies, impact on 245–6
   Black or socially marginalised 166, 171–3, 175–9, 181–4
   Enlightenment thinkers on 56–7, 58–9, 65–6, 75, 79–81
   gender roles, culturally determined 12–14, 112–13, 150–4, 185–9, 190–1
   historical distrust of 20, 28–34, 35–7, 41–4
   madwoman archetype 71, 86–7, 89
   marginalist economists on 111
   as mothers, *see* childcare; procreation
   multitasker archetype 185, *186*, 190–1

   sick leave data 145–50
   unpaid hours spent on care work 14, 16, 133, 134, 189
   urged to emulate men 21, 165, 179–80, 185, 193–4
   violence and discrimination against 23, 59–60, 113–14, 165, 173–4, 177–9
   workforce participation 142–5, 161–5, 184–5, 210–11, 245
'Women are a deficit to society' (*DR Nyheder* report, 2013) 3
'Women continue to be net expense for the state' (*Mandag Morgen* article, 2020) 3–4
Woolf, Virginia 195
workforce management, *see* human resources management
World Bank 18, 233, 247–8, 259
World War II, economics in 124–5

young people 198, 216

ABOUT THE AUTHOR

Emma Holten is a feminist activist and gender policy consultant. In 2014 she created the project CONSENT, raising awareness of digital sexual violence. Since 2019, she has worked with feminist economics. She served on the European Institute of Gender Equality Experts Forum as an expert in feminist economics, and on Human Rights Watch's advisory committee on Women's Rights. In 2023 she was appointed as advisor to the Danish government's investigation of power in Denmark. She has delivered keynotes at the Conference on the Status of Women at the UN, the Guadalajara Book Fair, the European Commission and many other places. She also has a degree in Modern Culture and has translated Chris Kraus and Silvia Federici. She lives in Copenhagen. *Deficit* is her first book.